MLI88078433

Love

x Theresa Gattuso O'Conner

A WHISPER FROM WITHIN

My Life, My Terms

THERESA GATTUSO O'CONNOR

WESTBOW
PRESS
A DIVISION OF THOMAS NELSON
& ZONDERVAN

Copyright © 2015 Theresa Gattuso O'Connor.

All rights reserved. No part of this book may be used or reproduced by any means, graphic, electronic, or mechanical, including photocopying, recording, taping or by any information storage retrieval system without the written permission of the author except in the case of brief quotations embodied in critical articles and reviews.

This book is a work of non-fiction. Unless otherwise noted, the author and the publisher make no explicit guarantees as to the accuracy of the information contained in this book and in some cases, names of people and places have been altered to protect their privacy.

WestBow Press books may be ordered through booksellers or by contacting:

WestBow Press
A Division of Thomas Nelson & Zondervan
1663 Liberty Drive
Bloomington, IN 47403
www.westbowpress.com
1 (866) 928-1240

Because of the dynamic nature of the Internet, any web addresses or links contained in this book may have changed since publication and may no longer be valid. The views expressed in this work are solely those of the author and do not necessarily reflect the views of the publisher, and the publisher hereby disclaims any responsibility for them.

Any people depicted in stock imagery provided by Thinkstock are models, and such images are being used for illustrative purposes only. Certain stock imagery © Thinkstock.

ISBN: 978-1-5127-0485-3 (sc)
ISBN: 978-1-5127-0487-7 (hc)
ISBN: 978-1-5127-0486-0 (e)

Library of Congress Control Number: 2015911705

Print information available on the last page.

WestBow Press rev. date: 09/04/2015

To my Amazing Husband Joe and my Beautiful Daughter Samantha,

I want to thank you both for giving me the glistening gleam to my eyes, in my Heart, Soul and Spirit. For showing me the will, awareness, strength, believing in me and never doubting my capabilities to overcome, whatever is in my way. That impossible is possible and that I can reach for the Highest Sparkling Stars in the sky and making my Dreams come true, one way or the other! "YOU BOTH ARE EVERYTHING TO ME IN THIS WORLD!" You two are my Miraculous and Magical Loves of my Life!!! I Love You Both Very Much!!!

CONTENTS

Introduction ix

The Day My Life Changed Forever 1

Jumbled Memories 14

Moving to A.I. DuPont Hospital for Children 17

Physical Limitations 20

Learning to Eat Again 24

Physical Therapy Helped Me Get Stronger and Learn
    to Walk Again 27

I Did not Want to Be "Handicapped" 30

Going Home from the Hospital 34

My Family Always Supported and Encouraged Me 36

Returning to School 43

Meeting Joe 46

I Did not Want to Be Treated Differently 52

Learning to Drive—the First Time 55

My Senior-Class Trip 59

Graduating from High School and Getting Married 61

God Tested Me—to See How Much I Could Handle 68

The "Mrs. New Jersey" Pageant 73

Joe's Parents Were Wonderful to Me 75

Missing the Freedom to Do Anything I Want 78

Don't Feel Sorry for Me 81

I Wanted to Go to Work 83

Dealing with My Father's Death 85

Having a Child 108

Finally Getting My Driver's License 122

Joining a Gym—and Being Told "You Don't Belong Here" 134

Discovering the "Healing Touch" 138

Going Back to Work 140

Going to College and Pursuing New Goals 150

Facing New Obstacles, Every Day 155

INTRODUCTION

MY NAME IS THERESA O'CONNOR, and this is the story of my healing after a brain aneurysm when I was only 14 years old. I am 40 years old now, and a lot of mostly wonderful things have happened to me since that terrible, life-changing day. I'm blessed that most of my life has been really happy, even since the aneurysm, though of course I've had challenges.

I'm writing this book because I want the world to know that people who are "disabled" or "handicapped" in some way are not *only* disabled. We're not even *primarily* disabled: we don't *define* ourselves by whatever medical problem we're dealing with. The rest of the world does that, but we don't. I'm a person, like everyone else—and not like anyone else. I'm a daughter, and a sister, and a wife, and a mother. I do as much as I possibly can.

Every day, I push myself to do more, because we all have only one life to live and I want to make the most of it. I did not let my aneurysm prevent me from finishing school, or getting married, or having a child, or having a job, or being happy. Other people tried to prevent some of these things, but this is the story of how I fought hard to have the best life I could possibly have.

THE DAY MY LIFE
CHANGED FOREVER

WHEN I WAS 14 YEARS old, my life changed dramatically. One day I was able to walk, run, speak out loud, and live life to the fullest, and the next day, I lost all ability to live independently. The first thing I remember after that terrible day is waking up in a hospital, after having been in a coma for two months, and I was confined and trapped inside my body.

My life-changing devastation occurred during Easter break from school, in 1986. My sister Joann and I were visiting our sister Linda, who was married and living in Salisbury, Maryland, on the eastern shore, about 100 miles from Baltimore and a little over 100 miles from Philadelphia. Joann and I are identical twins, we are the youngest of 10, and we are 9 years younger than our other brothers and sisters. Linda is the oldest, and she is 18 years older than I am. Then there's Marie, Julius, Rose, Grace, Andy, John, and Jimmy, who are all about 1-2 years apart, and then me and Joann. We all grew up on a big farm in Swedesboro, New Jersey, with about 72 acres, and even though my sisters and brothers were so much older, we were all very close, which is why Joann and I were visiting Linda that week.

Linda worked at the YMCA as a social worker, and I decided to go to work with her one morning, while Joann stayed back at the house watching our nephews, Michael, who was 6 years old, and John, who was 4. Linda and I drove to her workplace, and when I got out of the car, I felt kind of strange. I did not say anything to Linda, because I thought maybe I was just carsick. So she went to her office, and I was watching the kids in the daycare for a bit, when I felt this weird feeling in my head, something I had never felt before. It was very strange, and everything around me became blurry and fuzzy. I felt lost, as though my head had separated from the rest of me. I felt like I wasn't in my body, that I wasn't myself anymore. Then I had a splitting headache, and the pain was excruciating, but it came and then went away so quickly, which was really odd: I had never had a headache like that before. So I blew it off like it was nothing, but I still had an uneasy feeling.

About an hour later, Linda came by to see how I was doing at the daycare. She noticed I was acting kind of strange, so she told me she would take over so I could do something fun. She did not say anything to me at the time, but later she told me I had a really blank expression on my face, so she thought I was bored. I decided to go swimming for a bit, and then I went to the basketball court to shoot some hoops. I recall looking up at the basketball net and running toward it to do a lay-up…but I have no idea whether or not that ball ever went in, because the next thing I remember was being in Linda's office throwing up blood and complaining of a headache.

Linda rushed me to Salisbury Hospital (which is now called Peninsula Regional Medical Center). At first, the doctors thought I had a bleeding ulcer or that I was on drugs because there were a couple of other patients in the hospital with the same symptoms as I had. So they did not do any triage or any immediate care to see what the real diagnosis was.

I remember asking Linda, "Where's Joann?" and Linda told me Joann was back at the house watching Michael and John. But what she said to me did not register in my brain. I kept asking Linda the same question about Joann over and over again. All I wanted was Joann with me, and my mind just couldn't register that she wasn't. Before my aneurysm, Joann and I had been inseparable: we did everything together: we were both on the basketball team, we were both in the glee club, and we even did the Safety Patrol together for our School. If she did not go to school, I did not go to school, and vice-versa. We even wore identical clothes. We used to confuse our teachers, the principal, even our brothers and sisters sometimes, as a joke, to see if they could tell which of us was which. So when this happened, I wanted my twin sister with me, which is why I kept asking Linda where Joann was.

Meanwhile, Linda and the doctors kept asking me what was wrong, but I was slipping in and out of consciousness. Linda had called my mother to meet us at the hospital, and when she got there, I was unconscious. My mom tried to wake me, she even tried shaking me to wake up, and when I did not, she ran to get the doctors. That's when they realized I had fallen into a deep coma. It wasn't until hours later that they finally realized I had an aneurysm and the aneurysm had burst.

*   *   *   *   *

The next thing I remember is waking up from a deep sleep and slowly becoming aware of my surroundings. I was in a dark room, with harsh bright lights in the hallway that were streaming into my room through the open door. I did not know where I was: I knew I wasn't in my room at home, the room I shared with Joann, but nothing looked familiar. In front of me was a clock on the wall that said 2:00 o'clock. I guessed it was 2AM because it was so dark in the room. I tried to move my body but I wasn't able to. I thought to myself, *am I dead? I'm dead. I must be dead!* I did not know where I was. *Where is Mommy? Where is she? Where is everybody? How did I get here?* Then I heard a baby crying, and I tried to move my head to see where the baby was, but I wasn't able to do that either.

Then a woman came in, mumbling underneath her breath. She was very unpleasant and grumpy. She did not know that I had awakened from my deep sleep and that I was able to hear her. I did not know what she was doing to me. She kept rolling me from side to side. She was so rough with me, talking underneath her breath and

3

saying, "I can't believe I have to do this." As her voice became more enraged, she became rougher and more agitated with me. I could do nothing, literally: I was completely trapped in my body. I wasn't even able to communicate to her. *What is she doing to me?* I thought to myself. *Why is she so mean? Why is she changing me? Oh my Gosh! I am not wearing underwear; I am wearing a diaper!* I felt humiliated, and I wanted to say something so badly but I wasn't able to speak. Then I realized she was a nurse. As she rolled me for changing, I saw and heard the baby crying next to me. The baby was hooked up to so many machines. That was when I realized I was in the hospital. All the baby did was cry and cry. The crying was disturbing because all I wanted to do was close my eyes and sleep, to go to a place in my mind where I would wake up and all of this would be a dream. But that wasn't to be. I did not yet know what had happened to me, but I knew something terrible had happened.

I had been in a coma for almost two months, though I did not know that until later, of course. I had also been transferred from Salisbury Hospital to Children's Hospital of Philadelphia (CHOP) sometime in the first few weeks after the aneurysm burst. I did not remember any of this, but once I regained consciousness, my family told me some of what had happened. My sister Grace and her husband Luis were on their honeymoon in Hawaii, and my Mom called Grace right away: she wanted Grace to be with me because my Mom thought I wasn't going to make it.

When Grace and Luis received the phone call, it was the middle of the night. When my Mom told them how critical my condition was, they booked the next flight home. Grace told me later that everyone thought I was going to die and that she wouldn't see me alive again. As soon as they landed, Grace and Luis rushed as fast as they could to get to the hospital.

When Grace finally arrived at the hospital, her heart was racing a mile a minute as she hurried to find me and see me in my room, which was in the intensive care unit. Finally, Grace stood outside my room. My sister Rose told her to brace herself before she went in. When she walked in, she couldn't believe her eyes. She was so shocked, literally stunned and startled by how deadened I looked. My head was bald and all bandaged up. My skin was so pale. I wasn't able to breathe on my own, so I had a breathing tube down my throat. There were lots of other tubes going everywhere, including a feeding tube into my stomach. I had braces on my arms and legs to try to prevent them from curling in. When she saw all this, Grace told me she totally lost it. She couldn't grasp what had happened to me, and right then and there, she fainted. She literally passed out and fell onto the hospital floor. The next thing she remembered was waking up in a hospital chair, with Luis right beside her.

Another thing I found out later was that the hospital had given my entire family a room, so they could stay with me. The doctors told my family that the longer I stayed in a coma, the less chance I would have of surviving. They were devastated and their hearts were full of fear and apprehension. My Dad stayed for two weeks, and he left then only because he had to go back to work at DuPont. My sister Rose also went home, because she needed to get back to her teaching. While they were driving back home—it was a 2-1/2-hour drive—my Dad saw how upset Rose was, and he wanted to cheer her up, so he bought her an ice cream cone. I always thought that was so sweet. She did not want to leave, to go back to school and teach, but she had to. My Dad was very generous and very thoughtful at times: Rose also told me that right after Linda brought me to Salisbury Hospital, my Dad brought all my brothers and sisters chocolate Easter eggs to cheer them up, because they were all at the hospital with me on Easter morning

Two months after that Easter Sunday, I was still in a hospital. After my first awakening at 2AM sometime in late May or early June, I slipped in and out of a state of a semi-coma over the next few days. During that time, I heard and saw everything that was happening around me, but I couldn't respond in any way. Being in a coma for 8 weeks had totally changed my mental and physical states. I functioned like a 2-year-old in a 14-year-old body. This dramatic and horrifying experience was sickening to me because I was unable to communicate and unable to move any part of my body. I couldn't move my legs or my arms, not even a pinky. I couldn't hold or move my head. I was completely confined and trapped, and I wanted out! But I couldn't even communicate that, because I couldn't talk either.

What made this even worse is that I knew everything that was going on, and I remembered the people who came to visit me and the conversations they had with me.

I remember my Dad promising me that if I woke up and got better, he would send me to St. James High School instead of Kingsway. He knew that was where I really wanted to go after I graduated from St. Joseph's middle school. I remember my Mom crying and having tears coming down her face, and I felt so bad because I couldn't tell her I was OK.

I remember my friend Tiffany came to visit me. Tiffany and I had been friends since kindergarten: we always ate lunch together, we played basketball together; we did everything together. She was my best friend, and we always wanted to do things together. When she came to see me, she thought I was in a coma, but I was in a semi-coma, so I was aware that she was there. Somehow, I just felt her presence, but I couldn't communicate that to her. Tiffany's first visit made such an impact on me; it really hit me hard and is still so vivid in my mind today. She was crying, crying so bad, she was crying her eyes out. She kept saying, "This isn't Theresa. This is not Theresa." I was thinking, *Tiffany, it's me, I'm here. It's me, Tiffany.* I was actually screaming this in my head, trying to get her attention. But I couldn't talk to make her hear me; I had no way of communicating what I was thinking.

Then I thought to myself, *why is she crying so much? Do I really look that awful?* No matter how hard I tried, there was nothing I could do to get her attention. So while Tiffany was crying so much, I was thinking about the last time I had seen her, at my sister Marie's house. Marie had given Joann and me a huge 13th birthday party and had invited all our friends. So, when we saw each other at my birthday party, both of us ran toward each other, jumped into each other's arms, and gave each other a big hug. That was a year before my aneurysm: even though she was my best friend, we hadn't seen much of each other for a while because she had transferred out of the Catholic school we had been going to since kindergarten, and she was going to a public school called Clearview. As I lay in my hospital bed, I thought of the last time I had seen her, and all I wanted to do was to give her a big hug and tell her, *I'm still the old Theresa.* But the only thing I could do was watch her tears as she held onto my bed rail.

Another friend who came to see me was Tina Dombrosky and her sister Michelle. We've also been friends since kindergarten. In fact, we were born in the same hospital, two days apart: we were in the same baby ward together, Tina, Joann, and me. In my heart, Tina is more like a sister than a friend. To this day, she's one of my closest friends. I was in her wedding, and she was in mine. She has always stood by me, and that means the world to me.

So many of my friends came to see me while I was in the hospital: all my close friends from school—Lynn, Cathy, Donna, Tara, Jonathan, and so many others. I really appreciated everyone who came, because their visits cheered me up so much. I needed cheering up!

Another person who came to see me was a girl named Anne, whom I had met two years before my accident. She had been shot in the head at a gas station in Swedesboro, which is where I grew up. She came to see me because she wanted to make an impression on me. She could walk and she could talk; she was still struggling, but she was improving, and I think she wanted to give me hope because she was recovering from her trauma, I could recover from mine, too. All my friends were trying to support me, to bring me out of my coma and back to my old self.

I also have strong memories of my sisters showing their love and support for me, just by being there at my bedside, talking to me. My sister Rose was always there with me, and I often saw her crying and saying encouraging words and telling me she loved me so much!" But she also held my hand, trying to be strong for me. Rose was still living at home, with my parents and Joann. Also, Rose helped out with the house chores while my Mom was with me. Rose made dinner for my Dad, Joann, and my brother Andy, who was living home at that time, too. Sometimes, my Dad and Andy made dinner. Rose also helped get things situated with Joann: she washed and pressed her school clothes, and she made sure Joann was ready for school each day. Rose also fed Mommy's dog Muffin and all the cats on the farm. She really did a lot. Rose is 14 years older than I am, and she always helped out my mom when Joann and I were growing up. So we had a special bond.

I remember Rose saying silly things, to try to get a reaction out of me: one time she said, "Wake up, Theresa, and I'll make your favorite chocolate cherry cake." At that very moment, I wanted that cake so much. Then she said, "Or I'll make you my German chocolate cake." I remember thinking, *Rose, I don't like German chocolate cake. I want you to make the chocolate cherry cake: that's my favorite!* But I still couldn't react or move or speak.

I also remember visits from my sister Marie and her son Robert (who was 3 years old at the time). He did not stay very long, but I remember so vividly I was so happy within when he came to see me. I remember how my heart was so tickled hearing his precious voice; my heart felt so much lighter about my situation. He asked all kinds of questions about why I was sleeping and not waking up. I tried so hard to push out a reaction to reply back, but I was unable to respond in any way! I just enjoyed the time he was with me, and I listened to Marie replying to him, "Aunt Theresa will wake up, but she is not ready yet. She is just very tired, Robert." I watched Marie try to put on a happy face. I also remember Marie calling me "Sweet Pea" and telling me to "wake-up, Theresa, wake up," while tears were falling from her eyes and her lips quivered.

I remember Linda playing music for me on a tape recorder (though I don't remember what she played). I remember seeing

Grace at my bedside, being so strong for me and putting lemon swabs on my lips and rubbing my hand and feet to see if she could get a reaction out of me. I remember so vividly, she was telling me, "I love you, Theresa, I came back from Hawaii just for you, Sweetie. Wake up, Theresa, can you hear me?" Then she talked in a silly voice, trying to be funny, goofy, and whispering in my ear, telling me about the last memory she had of me at her wedding. Joann and I were having a ball and showing off our dance skills on the dance floor at her wedding and doing the Hokey Pokey. She giggled softly as she told me this, but she also had tears in her eyes. I just remember the glow in my heart and how happy she made me when she was there by my side.

I also remember Jimmy reading books to me and moving my legs and arms. I even recall Marie and Linda making a tape recording of everybody talking to me, which I never heard, but one of these days, I will listen to that tape recording! They tried anything to get me to wake up, but I was still in my semi-coma.

My brothers also tried doing goofy things to get my attention. One of my brothers put "The Three Stooges" on the television, for some reason. I did not know why he chose that particular show, but I remember thinking to myself, *Why is this show on, and why is the TV so loud?* I remember my brother Jimmy singing to me. One of the songs he sang was "The Impossible Dream. "I remembered the lyrics and sang them to myself over and over again. At the time, Jimmy did not know that his singing re-ignited the life force in my spirit and reawakened my mind. It gave me the courage and strength to come out of my semi-coma and feel alive again! What an impact and impression he made on me!

I also remember my brothers Andy and John and even my oldest brother, Julius, talking to me, reading stories, and talking really loudly, holding my hands and squeezing them, and telling me to open my eyes and wake up. I remember either John or Andy changed the channels on the TV and put on "Wrestle Mania" because they knew how much I loved watching that show. While the show was on, I remember thinking to myself, *are the wrestlers really fighting and wrestling for real, or is it all fake? Is it put on as an act?* Then John or Andy changed the channel to see what else was on, and I remember thinking to myself—and I wanted to say to them—*put it back on, I want to watch that show.* All I wanted to do was to take action and speak or move. But I wasn't able to do *anything* to get their attention since I still couldn't talk or move any part of my body. They were moving my arms and legs to see if they could get any reaction out of me, but nothing happened. I recall thinking, *why I can't I feel them moving them?* I so badly wanted to be able to move anything whatsoever.......

So many people came to see me—not just my immediate family, but aunts and uncles, too. My Aunt Jenny and my Aunt Jo, who were my mother's sisters, often came together to see me, once or twice a week. They always brought food for my Mom, and they always asked my Mom how I was doing, because they knew I still couldn't speak. They got lemon swabs from the nurses and swabbed all around my lips because they could see how dry my mouth was, and they knew that was a big treat for me. And they talked to me, asking me, "Can you hear us, Theresa? We love you, Theresa." They told me how my cats were doing on the farm and how my cats missed me, saying things like, "They want you to wake up so you can chase them all over the farm. They want you back home!" But I was still unable to reply back to them; I was so numb and baffled because I still couldn't talk. So I just laid there listening to what they had to say, and I had to hold everything in.

Although I was very frustrated because I couldn't communicate with my family, I was also so happy they were with me: I felt a warm and safe feeling inside me because they were there at my bedside.

I remember my Aunt Jenny promised me if I woke up, she would send me on a trip to Italy. She knew I wanted to go to Italy because that's where my mom's family is from: my Mom's maiden name is Musumeci. I wanted to wake up even if I couldn't go to Italy, but I still couldn't communicate that to anyone.

My Uncle Andy and Aunt Mary also came to visit me, and I was so excited when they walked into my room and I saw their warmhearted smiles on their faces. One day they brought me a card, and I wanted to open up the envelope so badly. But it felt like my arms and hands were chained up and I couldn't get them free to be able to use them again. It was such an unbearable task for me, so they finally opened the card for me.

Even the priest from my school came to see me many times. His name was Father Gary. He sat right beside me, next to my bed, and he always tried to talk to me with such positive energy and words. I still remember he always had a bright smile on his face to try to cheer me up and get some kind of a reaction out of me. He always brought me Snicker's bars and he said, "Theresa, I know you love Snicker's bars, so I'll just put them in your drawer for safekeeping: when you're ready to eat one, they'll be there. But don't forget they are there, OK, Theresa?" I remember just lying in bed because I did not have the strength or the knowhow anymore to respond, but I knew from within that I was so tickled he was there with me. Father Gary also brought lots of things that the kids at my school made me for me. They made beautiful cards that said, "get well" and "we miss you," and my Mom hung them on the wall in my room, so I could look at them.

I especially remember one visit from Father Gary very strongly because it made a very big impression on me. He brought a video tape that the kids had made for me: they were outside on the school grounds, talking and singing about wanting to me to get well because they wanted me back on the school basketball team, so I could kick butt against the other school's team. While I was watching the video tape, I had this striking memory of me playing basketball with my team at the Walter Hill School in Swedesboro. I was playing center and doing a lay-up when another girl elbowed me right on my nose, and she literally broke my nose! There was blood everywhere, all over the basketball court. They called a time-out to make sure I was OK. My coach, Mrs. Dombrosky, wanted me to stay out of the game, but I knew I had to get back in. She was an outstanding trainer, and she had taught me so many skills to improve my game, and I really respected her, but I knew I had to finish playing. Mrs. Dombrosky was a little hesitant, so she made sure it was OK with my Mom. My Mom asked me, "Do you want to go back in, Theresa?" And I said, "yes, I need to do this; this isn't going to hold me back from not helping my team to win the game. This girl who broke my nose is not going to pull me under and make me give up. I'm going to give it my all!"

There were only seconds on the clock for the game to end, and the girl who had broken my nose had the ball and she was dribbling down the court. I had such a driven power within me that without any hesitation or doubt, I just stole the ball from her, without making a foul. Then I dribbled the ball down the court, and I heard the crowd in the bleachers counting down the seconds for the game to end. I made a split-second decision to throw the ball at half court, and I couldn't even hear a pin drop while the ball was in the air going towards the basket.

Then I saw the ball go right into the basket: it was a complete *swish!* I did not even hit the backboard—the ball just flew right in. Everybody screamed and cheered, and my entire team was jumping up and down. Those were incredible moments for me—even though my team did not win the game. To me—and to my team-mates—we felt as though we had won because all that really mattered to my team was that I did not let my broken nose stop me or hold me back from finding my strength and giving it all to the game. Even now, as I'm writing and thinking about it, it's a great memory!

Then I remember seeing my Mom's face: how proud and ecstatic she was. But after the game was over, she rushed me to Underwood Hospital to get my nose checked out by a doctor, and sure enough, my nose was severely broken.

I recalled those incredible, thrilling moments when I watched the video tape the kids at school had made for me. It was so nice of them to make it, and it was so kind of Father Gary to bring it to me:

he will always mean a great deal to me. He was such an outstanding priest. He passed away a while back, but I will hold him and my memories of him in a dear and special place in my heart, forever.

Through the passing days, I was uncertain about so many things that were going on in my life at that time, but I somehow knew everything was going to be okay, because my Mom and family were right beside me. As long as I knew they were with me, I thought, *I can beat this and return to the way I used to be.* Most of all, I wanted my Mom to be present—and when she wasn't, I completely fell apart. She stayed with me 24/7.

I remember how distressed I was when she wasn't there. One time in particular comes to mind, as I was starting to wake up from a semi-coma, and I watched my mom as she walked into my room. I knew it was early in the morning because she was getting her clothes out and I saw soap in her hand. She went into the bathroom, and it seemed like it took forever for her to come out. I was so worried about where she was and when if she would come back out. I was so scared. I thought to myself, *why is she taking so long? Is she okay? Oh my Gosh! Is Mommy dead?* I remember I was crying inside. I was petrified! Everything was so stiff as if I were a heavy stone brick, unable to budge anything whatsoever. I wanted to scream, yell, and jump out of my skin. I just wanted to move about, but I could do nothing. I was constrained and locked up in my own body and I was becoming frantic. I couldn't figure a way out. I had to try to accept the fact that I couldn't move or speak—and just hope that my mother would return (which, of course, she did) and that I would eventually be able to get out of that hospital bed and be able to talk and function just like I did before my aneurysm burst. I was a long way away from that happening, though.

JUMBLED MEMORIES

DURING THOSE MONTHS WHEN PEOPLE thought I wasn't aware, I really did retain a lot of information and memories of my mom and dad, brothers and sisters, aunts and uncles, cousins, my friends and their parents, doctors, nurses, and really anybody who came to visit me. I remember one day when the nurse came to talk to my mom and dad in my room. They walked out of the room, but I could still see them talking to the nurse. Then a doctor in a white coat came in, and I remember feeling so scared as he told my mother he was going to put needles in my feet to see if I would be able to react or move them. I wasn't able to move my feet, but I remember thinking to myself *why can't I feel that?* They were having a very, very deep conversation. I knew they were talking about me and what was happening to me, and my parents looked so upset. I remember I just wanted to reach out to them, I wanted to talk to them and tell them *I'm OK, I'm here, I'm the old Theresa.* I wanted to reassure them, but I still couldn't talk. I still did not know myself what had happened to me, because I couldn't remember anything.

Then my memory started coming back: it was like something *sparked* in my brain. I began to recall so many memories, one after another: Playing basketball with my school team, playing basketball with my twin sister and with my brothers at home on the farm: I remembered the feeling of how much fun that was. We had a big farm, with sheep and pigs and a horse and about 20 cats and a few dogs. Then unexpectedly, my heart felt so sad because I remembered that one of Mommy's favorite dogs, Buttons, got killed when he was hit by a car in front of my house. I remembered that Joann had seen it happen: she was looking out the kitchen window, and she saw Buttons go across the road and get struck by a speeding car. She screamed when she saw that! I remember my heart felt so incredibly sad because I knew how much my Mom, Joann, and I—and even my Dad—loved Buttons. I loved all our cats, too, although my favorite was a gray cat named Smokey.

Then another thought came to my mind, and it felt like my mind was playing tricks on me because it came and went so fast. It was my brother John's wedding, when he got married to Lauri on October 1, and I was standing on a staircase at their reception at the Ramada, taking a picture and trying to be goofy and silly. Actually, my mind was going in all directions to grasp and trigger any kind of memory because I felt like my life was a flower fading away to worthlessness. I just wanted to embrace anything at all that came to mind.

The next thing that came into my mind was playing basketball, trying to block my brother Andy from shooting the ball into the basket that was hanging high on the barn. Then another significant memory came into my mind with a warm loving feeling, and I said to myself, *Oh my Gosh, Andy bought the basketball net as a Christmas present for Joann and me.* Then surprisingly, he hung it up onto the barn for us. When Joann and I came home from school, we were so excited to see the net hanging on the barn!

My mind suddenly recalled when my brother Julius took me for a ride on his motorcycle out in the farm field: we did not get very far because the motorcycle tipped over while both of us were on it. We did not get hurt, but I remember thinking, *whose bright idea was that?* But I did have fun!

Then all of a sudden, another memory was triggered in my psyche: it was a quick flash of me at my sister Grace's wedding, wearing the gorgeous light-petal-rose dress that my Mom bought for me and my twin sister. I was dancing on the dance floor at her wedding; then my mind switched back to when we bought the dresses at the mall.

I even recalled a memory of being in the car waiting for my Mom to come out of the grocery store at "Kings". She had parked next to a handicapped spot, and as I looked at it, I thought to myself, *I wonder how it would feel to be handicapped?* This happened just a few months before my accident, and I remembered thinking that would never happen to me, that I would never become handicapped—and certainly not at 14 years of age. I wonder now if that was a premonition, or just a coincidence.

Then I started dredging up bits and pieces of the last memories I had before this horrible calamity. I remembered that Joann and I were visiting Linda in Salisbury, Maryland on Easter break. I remembered being at the YMCA where Linda worked. I remembered playing basketball in the gym and looking up at the hoop, doing a lay-up to putting the ball into the basket, and then my mind went blank. I remembered being in Linda's office throwing up blood and complaining of a headache. I remembered being at Salisbury hospital, lying in the hospital bed, and asking Linda, "Where is Joann? "I remembered Linda answering me, "Theresa, Joann is back at my house, babysitting Michael and John." I remembered that I kept repeating the same question over and over again, "Where is Joann?" because I couldn't comprehend what Linda was saying and where Joann was. I remembered what had happened to me, and that was the worst memory of all.

MOVING TO A.I. DUPONT HOSPITAL FOR CHILDREN

AFTER I HAD BEEN AT Children's Hospital in Philadelphia for about 8 weeks, my parents decided to transfer me to A.I. DuPont Hospital for Children (AIDHC) in Wilmington, Delaware. They thought DuPont would be better for me, because it's a very good hospital and it was closer to where my family lived, so it would be easier for them to visit me than having to drive into Philadelphia, where CHOP was located.

I was transferred by ambulance, and my mom came with me in the ambulance; my sisters Linda and Joann followed, in another car. All I remember about that trip was being so thirsty in the ambulance, and I wasn't able to drink anything. My Mom and the nurse who accompanied me kept putting lemon swabs around my lips, but they did not quench my thirst. So the nurse thought it would be okay if we stopped at a Wawa to get a small carton of ice tea and I could drink a few sips out of a straw. I remember how it was so pleasing just to be able to have liquid in my mouth.

When I arrived at A.I. DuPont Hospital, it seemed different to me from any other hospital I had been in. It did not feel like a hospital. It felt more like a home: it had a kid-friendly atmosphere, and everybody felt like family. Everyone there showed kindheartedness, compassion, and thoughtfulness. The DuPont Hospital was only for children, not for adults. I knew in my heart that this was where I belonged from that time on, until I would be released from the hospital altogether. I did not know I would be there for almost a year, but on that first day, I felt at home. And to this day, I remain linked and connected to this warm and loving hospital.

I remember meeting my two primary nurses for the first time, Sharon and Fran. They were so incredibly kind and loving to me. They went above and beyond to make me feel so calm and *comfortable*. They gave me encouragement, faith, and hope that I could win my life- changing battle one way or another. They tickled my heart with their funny antics and jokes. Sharon did not even have to try. That was just her personality. Every time she walked into my room, my heart would glow. She always put a smile on my face, and she reassured me that everything was going to be okay.

Fran, my other primary nurse, was incredibly caring and loving too. She was very kind and attentive. I remember her soft-spoken voice and her calm attitude. She had composure and poise about her. She was a soft-hearted and amiable care provider and a motherly role model, and I will never forget her.

I also remember another nurse, Meg. A few days after I arrived at DuPont, my mom brought me into the bathroom and for the very first time, I looked in the mirror. When I saw how I looked, I screamed—but nothing came out because I still couldn't talk. I wasn't able to get my rage and anger out when the shock came and I saw that I did not have any hair on my head. My entire head had been shaved in preparation for the surgery after my aneurysm. The doctors at Salisbury Hospital had to drill into the right side of my head, just above my ear, but they shaved my entire head. Even though it had been two months, only about an inch of my hair had grown back; I wasn't bald, but my hair was so short, I might as well have been. Before my aneurysm, I had beautiful, long hair that fell almost to my waist. When I saw what I looked like with such short hair—and the scar from where they had drilled into my skull—I was so shocked that I just broke down and cried, and my tears streamed down my face for a long time. My Mom embraced me, holding me tight with her endearing love and soothing comfort.

Later that day, Meg walked in the room to check my vitals. When she leaned over me in my hospital bed, I was so consumed with rage at the sight of her beautiful black hair that I somehow was able to grab and pull her hair. I wanted her hair! I wanted *my* hair back! Meg was screaming, but I did not care. I kept trying to pull her hair.

Fortunately, for Meg, my mom, Jimmy, and Joann were there, and they pried my clenched hands out of her hair. I kept trying to say, "I want my hair back, – I want my hair back," but I had no ability to speak. The expression on my face showed how angry and upset I was. I looked up at my Mom with my tear-filled eyes while my body shook from a spasm. She held me while Joann and Jimmy held my legs and feet to stop the spasm. Then my Mom wrapped her arms around me, and her eyes were full of her own tears, while Joann kept saying to me, "It will grow back before you know it, Theresa. It will be long again. "I especially recall the reassurance and comfort in their voices. Then Jimmy said, in his deep, strong, confident, soothing voice, "Hey, kid, it's a 100% guarantee! It will grow back. It just takes time, Theresa!" And of course, it eventually did: now my hair is even thicker than it was before the aneurysm, and I'm also lucky that it completely covers my scar. But when I was 14 years old in that hospital bed, I did not know what was ahead of me; I only knew how miserable I was then.

PHYSICAL LIMITATIONS

OVER THE NEXT FEW MONTHS, I entered a state where I was able to move and blink my eyes to communicate with others. It was a state of instant release in my soul and spirit because I started to see the windows opening for me. My family and friends offered support by trying to guess what I wanted to say. They asked me *yes* and *no* questions and told me, "If yes, blink once and if no, blink twice." This went on for what seemed like an eternity! But at some point, due to sheer exhaustion, I stopped thinking of what I wanted to say. My thoughts would drift away and I would again fall into a deep sleep.

As I started to emerge from the comatose state, I was more aware of the efforts of the nurses and my family to physically move my body position. One day, the nursing staff, my doctors, my Mom and Dad, my brother Jimmy, and my sister Linda placed me on my side and put a small device under my ear. It was a little radio. Whenever I wanted to hear music, all I had to do was push the button with my ear! I thought that was totally great, but it was also a big challenge! I had no idea that it could be so difficult to move my ear, even just that small amount to push the button.

Other times, the nurses tried to sit me up in bed, which was a big fiasco because I wasn't able to move anything, nor could I hold up my head. I was very scared, anxious, and frightened at this time, as I realized that I was actually locked and confined inside my body.

I had to wear braces on both hands to keep my fingers straight, and the doctors had to put braces on my legs and feet because they had also begun to curve in towards each other. I was fed with a stomach tube, which was so very painful.

I also had a tracheal tube in my throat because I wasn't able to breathe on my own. I had been on a respirator-breathing machine for the first 6 to 8 weeks after the aneurysm burst. After the doctors took me off the breathing machine, they still left the tube in my throat because I was still unable to breathe well, and my throat and mouth muscles weren't moving yet at all. I was even unable to cough, which was another reason why I needed the tube because they had to suction my lungs to keep them clear. The nurses positioned me on my side so the doctor could put a tube down the trachea into my lungs.

I remember one difficult time when they were doing this and my sister Linda was holding my hand, squeezing it tighter and tighter while they were suctioning me. I remember her telling me, in a shaking and uneasy voice, "we need to get this done; I'll be right here with you. I'm not leaving you, Theresa." Getting suction was so severe and difficult: it was so painful, because my stomach tube would pull from my side, and the tube going down my throat would make me gag. It made me feel like I wanted to throw up, and the tube was so rough that it scraped the walls of my throat.

* * * * *

A few weeks later, I got pneumonia. It took weeks to get that under control, with respiratory and breathing treatments. Plus my trachea had a lot of scar tissue around it, which made it difficult to suction the excess fluids. After weeks of painful respiratory treatments, I started to get a bit stronger with my breathing and eventually, my doctors removed the tracheal tube.

I'll never forget that, because they had to take me to the operating room to do this. I was so frightened and scared. I did not know what to expect. I kept thinking, *Where is Mommy? Where is Mommy? Why isn't she here with me?* She wasn't there that day because she had something else to do; I don't remember what, but I did not blame her because she was there every other day, for all those months that I was in various hospitals. Linda was there in her place; still, I wanted my mom.

During the entire time, I was in the hospital—all the hospitals, in fact: Salisbury, CHOP, and DuPont—my mom stayed with me. She did not even go home at night: she always found someplace to stay in the hospital to sleep, or she slept by my bedside. The nurses always tried to convince her to go home, but she always buttered up the nurses so she could stay. She could have gone home, but because most of my brothers and sisters were grown up and had moved out of the house; the only ones who were still living at home were Rose and Andy, who were both in their twenties, and Joann, who was in high school, where I should have been, too! So my Dad and Rose and Andy were certainly capable of taking care of themselves and Joann, so that my mom could be with me. She basically lived at the hospital with me. She went home to check on things, to see if my dad and Joann were doing OK, but otherwise, she was there at the hospital every day. She was my rock: I always knew if she was there with me, I would be OK.

She also volunteered at the hospital, to help other patients. She helped my room-mate, Maria, who was totally paralyzed from the head down. She'd been this way since birth, and she was 16 when she was my room-mate. She was in bed all the time. So my mom tried to do whatever she could for Maria. Joann use to take Maria, in her bed, and pushing her all around the hallways, anywhere Maria wanted to go. I remember how happy she looked whenever Joann did this; she was so extremely loved, by my mom, sister and by my whole family and she was treated as though my family was her family, too. Maria's spirit was so alive and full of zest: she was truly beautiful, amazing and so incredible. She was my room-mate for the whole time I was there and we became very good friends.

My mom also helped another boy named Vern, who was paralyzed from the neck down. His parents had just left him at the hospital; the whole time I was there, I never saw them visit him once. So my mother fed him, changed him, made his bed, and acted like his mom. My mom was there for all the children who were in the hospital with me. I remember one night, though, when my mom couldn't stay with me, so my sister Grace offered to. She spent the night with me and made me feel secure and safe by sleeping beside me on a cot. The next morning, she had to leave, and I became very upset. I really did not want her to go and I started crying, but she had to leave for work. Grace's eyes teared up because she knew I did not want to be alone. She began to cry and apologized again for having to leave, gave me a really big hug, and then left. I could tell her heart was breaking as much as mine was because she had to leave. I continued to cry, and I remember my nurse Sharon consoled me and reassured me that everything would be okay. Sharon was such a sincere and nurturing nurse.

Then on the day when the doctors were going to remove my tracheal tube, I remember how anxious I was. Linda was with me and was trying to keep me calm, but I was still worried. I remember lying on the operating table with a sheet over me, wide-awake and waiting for the doctor. When the doctor came in, she looked at my neck and trachea. Her name was Dr. Padman, and she was a thin woman with a slender face and a warm smile, and she was wearing a long white medical coat. Her voice was so soft and delicate and calm as she said to me, "You'll be fine. You won't feel a thing. "She was so kind to reassure me that everything was going to be okay and that it wasn't going to hurt. Sure enough, when she took it out, I was completely awake, and it did not hurt! It strikes me as so interesting now, as I'm writing and thinking about this, so many years later. I was such a young girl going through this horrifying ordeal, but I always knew in my heart that I was in very good and qualified hands. What I realize now is that *I believed* in my own healing and had real faith back then, even through all my challenges and tribulations.

LEARNING TO EAT AGAIN

SHORTLY AFTER I ARRIVED AT A.I. DuPont, my doctors set up many therapies for my recovery: physical and occupational therapy, swimming therapy, speech and cognitive therapy, and of course, school.

When I first started physical therapy, the therapists placed me on my side and belly. All I remember was the agonizing pain I felt from my feeding cord pulling and tearing my stomach. Everything felt like it was being stretched, and it was complete pain and torture. But the support from my therapists, my nurses, my parents, brothers and sisters, relatives and friends reminded me that no matter what pain I had to go through, it would pay off someday when I would walk again. *No pain, no gain,* I told myself. I wanted to be able to walk again, of course, and although none of the doctors or nurses knew if that would be possible, they certainly weren't going to dissuade me from trying!

After the tracheal tube was removed, my speech therapist, Joy, began to teach me how to talk again and to eat. I had to retrain my mouth muscles first before I could actually start eating real food. This took quite a long time, but through speech and occupational therapy sessions and constant practice with those muscles, in four months, I was eating real food again! I remember how gratifying it was the first time I ate mashed potatoes! Boy, they were so especially good! I mean *really good!*

Another time, my sister Rose was pushing me in the wheelchair to the snack bar next to the cafeteria. We were looking at the vending machines, and Rose asked me if I was hungry. I shook my head yes, and I pointed to a can of spaghetti and meatballs. We sat at a table together and Rose opened the can. She was a little wary about me eating this, so she tried to cut it up into smaller pieces. She put the first forkful into my mouth, and it was so yummy and full of flavor. I thought those were the most scrumptious spaghetti and meatballs I had ever had! Rose saw the pleased and happy look on my face, but she was still concerned that I shouldn't be eating this. So she cautioned me, "Take your time and make sure you chew and swallow right. "I consumed every last bite. I'll never forget that meal because, during all the months before then, I hadn't realized just how famished I really was.

My hunger had become so bad, I had actually started dreaming about eating food. I remember nights when I would dream about food and about eating, and it felt so real that I woke up from a deep sleep. One time, I was dreaming about opening up a refrigerator and I saw all this food delicious food. There was fried chicken, hamburgers, fries, ice cream, and more. My ultimate favorite dish in the refrigerator was a big dish of spaghetti and meatballs. I was eating it and making a big mess with the sauce all over my lips and on my face. But, in my dream, I did not care! I just wanted to eat those spaghetti and meatballs! I was a hungry savage—so it was wonderful when I finally got to eat my favorite meal, even if it did come from a hospital vending machine!

Food was always on my mind, mostly during the day, because my roommate Maria ate breakfast, lunch, and dinner on her side of the room, and I could see her eating. I was so jealous! Her mother, grandparents, and Aunts were so sweet but they would bring in food lots of times. Especially, from McDonald's, and the scent of those French fries and hamburgers made me want them so badly. The smell drove me crazy. I remember thinking that they were being cruel, but then I pushed that thought out of my head, because I realized they had no idea what I was feeling, and they weren't doing anything to make me feel bad intentionally.

While I was at DuPont Hospital, food was really my focal point. It had to be re-introduced in stages, like baby food: first, I could only eat well-ground food, then well chopped, and then I began to eat solid food. My family brought in homemade food. My sister Marie brought me desserts she had made that were out of this world. One time, she brought me her homemade chocolate cake, and it was absolutely the most scrumptious cake I had ever had. Whatever food she made for me was incredibly delectable and delicious. I really looked forward to the days when she came to see me.

There were also lots of times that my sisters bought me food from the cafeteria. I loved that, too, because they bought me fries and a hamburger or milkshake—pretty much whatever I wanted. One time, my sister Grace brought in strawberry popsicles, and I was so excited! Then, after I had eaten one, I broke out in hives that were terribly itchy. Later, the nurses and my mom realized the hives resulted from the strawberry popsicles, so I've never had a strawberry Popsicle since! But while I was eating that strawberry Popsicle, it was so remarkably good! And fortunately, as the weeks passed, my mouth muscles got stronger, and I wasn't watched as closely when I ate.

PHYSICAL THERAPY HELPED ME GET STRONGER AND LEARN TO WALK AGAIN

AT THE SAME TIME THAT I was working on relearning how to eat, I was also involved with intense speech, occupational, and physical therapy twice a day. I was getting stronger every day. My therapists put me between the parallel bars, to try to teach me to hold myself up and to take my first step. I remember the first time when I actually took my first step holding onto those parallel bars. I did not know whether I wanted to cry or laugh hilariously. I was so elated! I was on cloud nine! That moment will always be unforgettable in my mind. Everybody in the therapy room was cheering, clapping, and overjoyed! One of my physical therapists, Debbie, was behind me and holding onto me, and the assistant therapist, Vinnie, was in front, spotting me just in case I fell or collapsed onto the bars. They were encouraging me, saying, "Theresa, you can do this – you can do this – come on, Theresa, take another step. Don't give up! Push yourself! You can do this! Theresa, come on!" Somehow, someway, I got focused and I did. I took another step! My therapists were amazed.

A few minutes later, they brought my Mom into the room to see me. The feeling I felt was one of power and excitement as Mom watched me walk between those parallel bars, actually moving my legs for the first time. I don't remember when this was—my time at DuPont Hospital is a blur, but I remember that day vividly. My body was actually quivering from head to toe. When my Mom saw me walk, her face lit up like a sunbeam, her eyes glimmered so brightly, and her smile was luminous. Her reaction ignited in me the desire to do my very best: I felt every fiber of my inner self and mind that *I will defeat this.* My Mom gave me such a strong assurance of hope, faith, and encouragement that I would persevere over this: I would never give up on myself. She gave me the biggest hug, and she assured me, with a quiver in her voice, that "You are not alone. I am with you every step of the way, Theresa. I believe in you! You can and you will conquer this! I LOVE YOU- I AM SO PROUD OF YOU!" It was this assertive assurance from her that allowed me to believe in myself and reminded me that with hope, faith, and perseverance, I would get better and walk again. I would never give up on myself with Mom, Dad, and my family by my side.

I also did swim therapy. I had been a great swimmer before the aneurysm burst, so I really enjoyed swim therapy, and after two years of it, I got pretty good again. But I'm getting ahead of my story.

After so many weeks of intense therapies, my hands and fingers were also getting stronger. They weren't as curled, and I was able to straighten them enough to steadily hold a spoon or fork to feed myself. So one evening, my sister Rose came to see me, and she decided to take me to the third floor of the hospital, where there was a place called "Child Life," where patients could do all kinds of activities and crafts. Rose and I kept debating what we should do there. I came up with the idea that I wanted to make a bracelet out of beads for my Aunt Jenny.

Making the bracelet was tremendously difficult. I remember how complex and challenging it was to hold the bead and straighten my fingers to put the bead into the thread. What a task it was! My head was spinning, but I was so proud of myself, and I couldn't wait to give it to my Aunt Jenny, which I did a few days later. The expression on her face was unforgettable and reflected how really happy she was because of the progress I had made in regaining the use of my hands. Aunt Jenny said my gift was a "golden treasure" and she would treasure the bracelet forever and ever. Her response felt like much more than just a "thank you":it was an opening of her heart and love, and it triggered a spark within me that warmed my inner core and reassured me that I would heal and get better. Today, my beautiful Aunt Jenny still reminds me how much the bracelet means to her and how special it is to her heart!

I DID NOT WANT TO BE "HANDICAPPED"

AFTER THE ANEURYSM BURST IN my head, it did not only change my life; it also changed my relationship with my twin sister, because I saw myself—or how I used to be—in my twin sister. We had always been two peas in a pod: we did everything together. We were inseparable. What she wore, I wore. Whatever sports she played, I played—especially the sport of basketball, which we loved playing. We were on our school's basketball team, and we loved competing against other teams. We loved the thrill of competition! A few times, we even tricked our coaches and switched shirts because the only way our coaches could tell us apart was by the numbers on our shirts! Joann and I got a kick out of it: we thought it was funny, but I don't think our coaches always did. Joann and I especially loved playing against our brothers. It was thrilling, exciting, and very satisfying the times when we actually did win. We shared an amazing bond of closeness that only twins can understand, and we believed that nothing would ever tear us apart.

But after the aneurysm burst, I was so devastated and angry towards Joann: I was bitter and very jealous of her. Every time I saw her, I saw myself, and it was so frustrating to see her doing all of the things I had been able to do at one time in my life, but now that was all gone, in the blink of an eye. I once was physically able bodied, not limited, and then suddenly, I was totally limited, and so much was taken away from me. Joann told me I was very mean to her during that time in my life. I did not mean to be mean to her, but I was only 14 years old when this happened, and it seemed as though my entire life was taken away right from under me, and I felt literally imprisoned and trapped inside my own body with no way to get out and be free again. I just wanted my physical mobility back and to be normal again—how I used to be. I was angry! I wasn't really angry with Joann, because it wasn't her fault for what had happened to me; I was just angry in general, and because Joann was my twin and I saw her continuing to live her life the way I wanted to live mine, I took much of my anger out on her. I hope this book clears up why I was so mean to her and gives Joann a bit of clarity of what I was going through back then... and that I still am going through to this day.

I remember one time my mom came to the hospital and told me we were going to Sea Isle City for the weekend. I asked where Joann was, and my mom said to me that Joann and Rose were already at the beach. When we got there, my mom was pushing me in my wheelchair on the boardwalk, and I saw Joann running on the beach and talking to the lifeguards. She was having fun, being free, playing Frisbee. And I remember thinking, *last summer, I was on that beach with Joann, playing football with a couple of boys we met, being free, walking along the ocean together, and having fun. And now I'm in a wheelchair.* I was very bitter and very angry because I couldn't do anything. I couldn't even talk that well yet: I was still talking in only a whisper. I was so angry. I wanted my mobility back. I wanted to get out of that wheelchair. My mom thought she was doing something nice for me—and I know she meant well—but it was so painful for me to watch Joann doing what I wanted to do, what I used to do, and realize that I might never be able to do those things again.

It took lots of time and soul searching within myself before I could face the fact that I am handicapped, and before I could love myself and be proud of who I am. When I overcame that battle in my mind, it made me accept myself and made me realize other important qualities to focus on, which enabled me to move forward with my life and be happy with my twin again, and with others.

Overall, that acceptance gave me a much more powerful and positive outlook on life. Yes, my life is still very hard at times, but acceptance of my situation has ignited a flame within me to rise above and reach the unreachable of where I want to be in my life. I want to achieve my goals and dreams. I want to persevere and believe and never give up on myself, so I can become a very strong person. The clarity helped me find the power of my core from within, which gave me a better understanding to fight even harder when confronting my obstacles, hurdles, and battles. I see the whole picture of what my life is all about and the plans God has for me. He's giving me the strength and courage of what I need to do in my life's mission. I know without a doubt in my mind that even though I have a disability, even though I still have trouble with my lower and upper extremities, and even though I use a wheelchair, I *believe* and *have faith* that God is holding my hand, guiding me every step of the way to enlighten me and enrich my life in so many other ways!

Before my aneurysm, I wasn't overly religious, but I believed in God, and I went to church, though not every Sunday—maybe only two or three times a month. I went to Catholic school. In fact, all my brothers and sisters went to Catholic school, though to this day, I don't know how my parents were able to afford it, with 10 kids! But they did, somehow. I also enjoyed reading the Bible. Before the aneurysm, from when I was about 8 or 9 years old, I used to come home from school, go straight up to my mom's bedroom, and get out her bible. It was a big, beautiful bible, and I would lie on her bed and read it. .

I always knew that God had my back, which He would always be there for me. It's taken me many years to come to terms with this, though, and when I was still a teenager, I certainly did not always feel this way. When I first realized I was going to be handicapped for the rest of my life, I cried my eyes out; I did not want to be handicapped. I wondered, how was I ever going to move forward in life? How would I ever be happy? For a long time, whenever I heard the word *handicapped*, I started to cry, uncontrollably: my situation and that word were so detrimental to my emotional and mental states at times. That was the hardest thing to do—for me to accept my situation.

GOING HOME FROM THE HOSPITAL

AS I GOT BETTER, I could go home on the weekends. I was so excited about that! The first time I went home, it was only for a day, but soon I could go home for an entire weekend. My parents came to pick me up, and one of my physical therapists showed my parents how to put me in the car, how to get my legs in the car, how to fold my wheelchair, and how to put it back together.

The first time I was allowed to go home for a day wasn't until the end of August, and I had been in the hospital since March. Everybody was there—all my sisters and brothers and their families, too. It was incredible. I remember my brothers Andy John and Jimmy helping me out of the car, getting me into the wheelchair, and pushing me next to the picnic table under a tree I loved so much. That tree was so full and flourished with bright, colorful green leaves; it had been planted years earlier, when the rest of my siblings were little. I was so excited to see everybody, and I was also happy to see all my cats, especially my favorite cat, Smokey, and my dog Muffin.

My mom had made such a beautiful dinner for me: it was a typical Italian dinner of spaghetti with meatballs, sausages, and meat sauce. I thought it was the greatest dinner ever. We ate in our big family farm kitchen, and it was just so nice to be away from the hospital and be home and do something normal with my entire family.

I came home permanently about a year after the aneurysm burst. My parents made a few changes to our house: I had a bed that was automatic in the back room, where I stayed for a while. Eventually, I moved back into the room I shared with Joann because there weren't enough bedrooms in our house for me to have my own room. I was mostly in a wheelchair, but I also had a walker, so I just managed without any ramps or any other special handicapped stuff.

We had a two-story house, and either my mom or my dad helped me walk or carried me into the house. I was even able to walk upstairs, though very slowly and very carefully, and usually someone was behind me in case I fell. I held on to the walls, the railings, whatever I could. I just did what I had to do; I always figured out a way to be able to do whatever I needed to do. My mom used to walk with me to the bathroom: once inside the house, I used my walker, not my wheelchair. I was very scared of falling, and I did fall, a lot, but I just picked myself up and tried again. I did not want to accept myself as handicapped then. I wanted help, but then again, I did not want help.

MY FAMILY ALWAYS SUPPORTED AND ENCOURAGED ME

MY MOTHER, FATHER, BROTHERS, AND sisters—even my aunts, uncles, and cousins—surrounded me and never gave up hope for me after I became physically disabled. They all believed in me, that I would overcome and conquer this, one way or another. All my siblings, each and every one were the main people in my life who helped me see the importance of hope and faith and believing, and they all encouraged me to never give up. Linda, Marie, Julius, Rose, Grace, Andy, John, Jimmy, and Joann showed me so much support, encouragement, and overwhelming love. They gave me determination and motivation and told me, "You can do it, Theresa, you can!"

I did not always appreciate their encouragement, unfortunately—especially while I was still in the hospital. My sister Rose reminded me recently that I threw a tube of toothpaste at her one time when she told me to stop feeling sorry for myself. I had trouble brushing my teeth, because it was hard for me to put my hand up to my mouth. She said I threw the toothpaste so hard that I hit her nose, and she still has a bump on her nose. I guess I had some strength, to throw it that hard, but I only seemed to have that kind of strength when I was angry or very emotional. Another time when I was in the hospital, I was mad at my sister Grace because I had a really hard time lifting up the blow dryer to dry my hair and I wanted her to do it, but Grace wouldn't. I got so mad at her and so frustrated with myself that I threw the hair dryer at her. To this day, Grace reminds me every now and then about that tantrum episode of mine.

On a more positive note, Marie reminded me what she did for me when she took me, Joann, and her daughter Christine shopping, and she decided to park in a handicap spot without a handicap placard. When Marie got out of the car, a woman approached her and said, "You sure don't look like you're handicapped." Marie blew her top and said, "Lady, my sister is in the car, and she is handicapped and needs a wheelchair. She can't walk, unless she uses a walker. So don't automatically assume about others until you know the facts, lady." Marie told me that story again recently, and she still gets upset about it because she knows what I go through every day, in so many different situations, and she knows people still make assumptions about my disability.

When I came home permanently, my Mom and Dad threw me a welcome-home party at the St. Joseph's Hall in my home town of Swedesboro. All my family and lots of my friends were there. That party was so very special to me.

*   *   *   *   *

I wanted to do sports, to go out and do a lot of things that other teenagers were doing, but I couldn't do. While my friends were joining the basketball team or the track team, or even going out to the mall, I couldn't do any of that. While they were out riding bikes or skateboarding, I was home watching a lot of TV. I remember how hard that was especially when it was a beautiful day outside, bright and sunny. I did not want to stay in on those days, so I would try to walk outside, with my walker. If my mom was busy doing something, I would sneak out the front door. But there was a high step down from our front door. I remember stepping down so very carefully, holding on to the railing, and dragging my walker down with me. I was so happy when I did this without falling!

But I only tried a few times, because it was really hard to do. One time I went out to our greenhouse, and all the kittens were out there. I remember my cat Smokey following me and my walker. And eventually, someone would come and find me. Daddy caught me once, and I was so relieved that he wasn't mad at me; he just wanted to make sure I was OK.

When I was home, my brother Jimmy often helped me walk outside in the farm's field, letting me hold onto his arm. Sometimes, he tried to make me walk by myself, and I was so scared because it was so extremely hard. Every now and then, I got so mad and told him, "I quit! I can't do it, Jimmy!" I got so frustrated with myself because it was really rough and hard to keep my balance. But Jimmy always replied back, "Yes, you can, Theresa! Fight, Believe! Stay positive and push yourself, kid! You can do it!" Jimmy pushed me even harder when I wanted to give up, and I wanted to cry my heart out, but I believe his determination helped me refocus and made me even stronger, knowing I could do this and walk through those fields at times holding with or without Jimmy's arm. I actually felt powerful, and he made me realize that I was not a quitter. I could persevere and strive to reach my goals and dreams. He helped me see the light shining from the mountain tops that I wanted to climb. With his help and encouragement, I knew that nothing was impossible.

Jimmy really encouraged me a lot. He even got me a treadmill. He bought it with his own money, and back then, those treadmills were really expensive. He was so kind to me—and so encouraging.

Another time, Jimmy and I had a funny but not-quite-funny moment when he decided to take Joann and me out to the movies: he wanted to take us for a ride in his new car that he had just bought. It was a used car, but it was new to him, so he wanted to show it off. Joann and I were excited he was taking us out, she helped me get into the front passenger seat. As Joann got into the backseat, Jimmy got into the driver's seat and then said, "We have to stop over my friend Ron's house." We said "ok", but then the car had trouble starting up.

Jimmy tried a couple of times to start the ignition; finally, it started running. Joann and I were so happy about that because we wanted to go out and see a movie with our brother. Since I spent so much time at home, it was a real treat to get out. That's why I was so happy when Jimmy finally got his car started so he and Joann and I could go to the movies. So we were heading to his friend Ron's house when all of a sudden, the car felt like it was slowing down, and it got to a point where the engine was shaking and the car was stalling. The car kept stalling, but we managed somehow to get to Ron's house. I waited out in the car while Joann and Jimmy went into Ron's house. When they all walked out of the house, Jimmy opened the hood so he, Ron, and Joann could look at the car engine and try to figure out what was wrong with it. My brother had this bright idea that it might need oil, so he put oil in the engine and got into the driver's seat to start the engine. When he started the ignition, the car engine caught on fire, with huge flames. I still remember that moment in time because Jimmy ran so fast out of that car like a chicken with skates on, and so did Joann and Ron. Meanwhile, I was stuck in the car because I wasn't able to get out and run!

When they had gotten far enough away from the car, Jimmy and Joann finally realized "we forgot Theresa! Oh, my Gosh!" Jimmy ran back even faster than he had run away from the car. In the blink of an eye, he swooped me up out of the passenger seat and carried me quite a distance away from the car. Jimmy put me down on the grass and said, with a smirk on his face, "Theresa, you could have been burnt toast." With a sly giggle, I said, "Really, Jimmy, I love you too."

While Jimmy was always positive in the way he encouraged me, my sister Grace is absolutely amazing but supported me in a different way: she gave me no pity at all. Joann and I often stayed over her house for a weekend, and if I needed help getting off the couch or getting dressed, or if I wanted a snack in the kitchen, she wouldn't help me. Instead, she always told me, "Theresa, come on, you can do it. I'm not helping you, because I know you can do this on your own." She actually made me cry, and when I told her "No, I can't do this!" she said, "Theresa, yes, you can, I am not going to feel sorry you, and I am not going to give in to you because I KNOW YOU CAN! I have all the time in the world, and I'll wait until you accomplish what you need to do."I remember my stomach was so twisted inside and I wanted to wring her neck because she was so enormously tough and stubborn with me.

But after all those times that Grace was being resilient and challenging with me, I hark back to how enthusiastic and wound up and stimulated I was after those daunting challenges that I overcame. I knew deep down Grace meant well and she wanted what was best for me. I was so fulfilled and uplifted after accomplishing those hurdles of mine. She made my deadened spirit and soul breathe again with hope, faith, and liveliness again. Grace knew that my will was already there to find my power and to commit myself to never give up on myself. She wanted me to realize that and embrace that power! I remember the tenderness, and the empathy and the concern in Grace's face and how she was so proud of me.

Grace did not always make me cry; she also appreciated the humor in some of the things that happened to me. One time in particular comes to mind when Joann and I stayed over Grace and Luis's house for a weekend. It was late on Saturday night, and we had all gone to bed. I was alone in the bedroom, across the hall from Grace and Luis's bedroom. I decided to try to do some exercises in bed, so I decided to Indian sit—which I did, but then I fell out of bed, upside down on the floor, with my legs up in the air. I did not know whether I should laugh or cry. So I called for help! Joann heard a faint cry, but she was in the bathroom, so she couldn't come right away. Grace and Luis thought they were hearing things because my cry was so faint, then they realized it was me. All three of them came into my bedroom, and when Grace saw me upside down with my legs up in the air, she burst out laughing, and then we all chimed in with her and laughed. It must have been a very funny sight, to see me upside down on the floor next to the bed. Grace said, "I certainly did not expect that, and if I ever want to crack myself up, I'll just think about that!"

Luis was also incredibly supportive of me: he never gave up hope on me. He is such an exceptional brother-in-law; in fact, in my eyes, he was and now will always be my extraordinary and amazing brother. He made my world back then so much more vivid, and he really lifted my spirits. He was always trying to brighten my day, improve my attitude, and encourage me with his positive outlook on life and supportive words. He always would tell me, "NOTHING IS IMPOSSIBLE. You can do whatever you want; I believe in you, Theresa, and you need to believe in yourself! Believe your dream!"

One day, Grace and Luis got me a plaque that said "The Power Within." I'll never forget what it read. It will always be a keepsake in my heart, especially when I'm feeling lost and overwhelmed. But the most special thing that Luis did for me happened on the one-year anniversary of my life-changing ordeal, and I will never forget it. I was at A. I. DuPont for school and for therapy. After I was done with my therapies, I went to see my Mom, and Luis was waiting with her in the volunteer lounge. He had come because he knew how difficult and disturbing this day was going to be for me, and he wanted to make it as special as he could, so it wouldn't be a sad day.

Luis took me out to lunch, to a restaurant where my Mom always took me after my various therapies: we went there to get me ice cream. That was always such a big treat for me, and my mom knew how special that was for me, and because I absolutely loved ice cream, my Mom would always try to go above and beyond to make me happy. Before we got out of Luis's white Camaro, he leaned over the backseat and grabbed a bouquet of beautiful white roses. He handed them to me and said, "These are for you, Theresa. You are as beautiful and bright inside and out, just like these white roses. Hold strong, be brave, and don't give up. I don't know why this happened to you, Theresa, but there is a reason why; everything happens for a reason, and it may not be tomorrow or years from now, but sooner or later, you will find your answers."

Tears were streaming down my face, happy tears and sad tears, but my heart was so tickled by Luis helping me get through this difficult day. He made my heart stronger, and he regenerated a spark within me that I would overcome this one way or another. Then he held out his arm to me, to help me walk over to the picnic table, and we sat outside that restaurant and had a lovely lunch and ice cream, on a sunny, beautiful day. Luis changed that horrible day of all days into such an exceptionally amazing day, and I will always cherish in my heart the memory of his kindness to me that day.

* * * * *

My mother and father, though, were the two people who gave me the most courage and strength to go on! They were great examples for me in how to live and work hard. I saw it in their eyes, and I saw it through their inner strength, because they never gave up hope that I would recover from what happened to me. They had to work really hard for the things they wanted in life, most of which was to provide for and to take care of their ten kids. They shared with us the motivation, the determination, the perseverance, and most of all, the confidence and pride required to keep on going and not to give up or to be discouraged.

My mom and dad taught me that you have the power within yourself: the power within your heart. They showed me that you can conquer and overcome any battle or barrier that is in your way. This is the reason that I have survived my disability. They gave me strength to continue on. Yes, I had my good and bad days, but I put my faith in God and played the cards I had been dealt. God knows how much I can handle and will never let me down, even if sometimes I think I am given too much!

RETURNING TO SCHOOL

I SPENT TWO YEARS OF my life in AIDHC relearning everything: how to walk, how to talk, even how to eat. In addition to all my therapies, I had school there every day for what would have been my first two years of high school. I was living at home then, but I went back and forth, as an outpatient. My mom took me there every day.

It wasn't a regular school day. I went to school in the morning, then I had physical therapy, then school again, then occupational therapy, then swim therapy, and then speech therapy. Even though I had only a few hours of school each day, the teaching was one-on-one, so we were able to cover everything that students in regular schools were learning. I had the greatest teacher, Tom Sicoli, who worked with me on everything: science, history, English, math, even Spanish. I loved learning from him because he was incredible. He encouraged me and supported me, and he became one of my closest friends.

There were other kids who were also in school: I was in a classroom with kids of all different ages, but there was a teacher and an assistant for each child. It was a great way to learn, and I did not feel lonely or isolated because all the other kids there were also recovering from some injury or illness, just as I was. I made friends with one girl, named Kim. She was about a year younger than me, so we naturally were drawn to each other because we were so close in age. She had been in a very bad car accident, and she couldn't walk for a while. She had also lost one of her eyes, but they gave her an artificial eye. And she learned to walk again.

As I mentioned, I went to school at DuPont Hospital for two years, when my teacher told me he thought I was ready to go back to a regular high school, for 11th grade. He was absolutely right: I was ready physically, but a part of me did not want to leave AIDHC because it had become my second home. It was my safe haven, and nobody there treated me any differently just because I had a disability. They saw me as *me*, not a person in a wheelchair. I was so scared to go back to high school, but I knew I had to face the real world and attend Kingsway Regional High School, back in Woolwich Township, New Jersey.

I wanted to go to Catholic High School, but it did not have an elevator, so I couldn't go there. That was one of my dreams, but God saved me, because if I hadn't gone to public school, I would never have met Joe. I'm getting ahead of my story again.

The first day I went to high school, I felt different, out of place, like I did not belong. It was so hard because I saw all my friends running around, doing whatever they wanted to do, with no limitations at all. I was so closed up inside and very depressed because I was in a wheelchair and not able to do the things I used to do with my friends. To make things even worse, some of my friends did not even speak to me. I remember one girl, who had been my friend for years, did not even acknowledge me. To this day, I don't know why she couldn't just say hello. I guess she did not know how to react to my being in a wheelchair, but still, I would think she would have had the decency to at least come over and say hi. Also, even though I was with Joann, she did not know anyone either. She had been going to the Catholic high school, but when we realized I wouldn't be able to go there because they did not have an elevator, Joann said she wanted to be with me, so she decided to transfer to the public high school with me. I think it was even harder for Joann than for me, because all her friends were at St. James, and she sacrificed that to be with me. So she needed to make all new friends, and apparently, I did, too.

That first day was very, very hard. It was so bad that when I got home from the bus, my mom and dad were outside waiting for me. My dad came over to help me off the bus: he picked me up, and right then and there, I put my arms around him and I just cried and cried. I looked over at my mom and saw that she also had tears in her eyes, but she knew she had to be strong, and she kept wiping the tears off her eyes down her cheek so quickly so I wouldn't see her cry. She knew this was only the beginning of what life challenges would lay ahead for me and what I would need to overcome in the future.

The next day, I did not even want to go back to school. I wanted to go back to DuPont, where everybody was the same as me and where people did not treat me differently. I felt like such an outcast in the beginning when I went to Kingsway High School. But I couldn't go back to DuPont, so the next day, I just forced myself to go back to Kingsway.

I don't know if my teachers said anything to the kids before I came back to school. To make things even worse, they had put me in special classes, which they thought would be easier for me--especially English, and I loved English class! They did not even test me when I came back. They just assumed I would need easier classes because of what had happened to me. I did not, though: I was fine mentally, and the classes they put me in were so easy that I was soon bored again. I realize they probably had good intentions, but I did not need any more boredom in my life!

MEETING JOE

A COUPLE OF DAYS LATER, I met Joe O'Connor, and my whole life changed. He was the first person in high school I was able to open up to, and he soon became my high-school sweetheart (and my husband, but that's getting ahead of my story!). We just connected with each other instantly. He helped me fit in to my new surroundings, and he soon became my entire world. He was my prince, always there for me, no matter what, encouraging me to follow my dreams. In his eyes, he saw the beauty within me.

I had seen him around: he was skinny, about 5'7" or 5'8" (I'm 5'5" or 5'6"), and he had short, light-brown hair. He was trying to grow a mustache and a beard, but there was just a little bit of hair on his chin and above his lip. I thought he was cute, but I did not know who he was. Joe had noticed me, too: he saw Joann walking in the hallway one morning, and that afternoon, he saw me in the wheelchair, and he thought Joann and I were the same person. We still looked very much the same, in the way we dressed and in our hairstyles, so he did not realize there were two of us; he just thought we were playing a joke. This happened for a couple of days before Joe said anything to either one of us. Then one day Joe approached me in Study Hall and asked what was going on: "I see you walking in the morning, then you're in a wheelchair in the afternoon: what gives?" With a gleam in my eye, I said, "that was my twin sister walking, but I am a lot sweeter!"

My sister Rose was at my school that day (I don't recall why), and she saw Joe and me talking, so she came up to me and asked,

"Who is this guy you're talking to?" (All my siblings were always very protective of me.) I introduced her to Joe, then I started to get out of the wheelchair, and Joe helped me into a regular chair, which was really sweet of him, especially since he had just met me. Then he jumped into my wheelchair and started doing wheelies. I laughed my head off when he did that, because no-one had ever done that before.

We just hit it off: we just clicked right then and there. He asked me why I was in the wheel chair, and I told him what happened to me. When I mentioned my twin sister, he told me he had almost approached Joann that morning and asked her out. But then he approached me in the afternoon instead. I was lucky he hadn't asked out Joann! Later, Rose told me she thought he was very, very nice. He was very sweet and very encouraging of me, ever since that day we met. He waited for me after school every day. He would leave class early and wait for me at the end of the day, until my mom or dad picked me up. I would be in class, and Joe would walk by and make a face in the window in the door, against the glass. He wanted me to know he was there for me, that he was thinking about me. He was very goofy but also very attentive and very loving, right from the start and because one of my parents drove me to school and picked me up at the end of the day, Joe met them right away. I remember when I introduced Joe to my Dad, Joe shook my dad's hand: he wanted to make a good impression on both my parents.

My parents were happy for me that I met Joe. I know they wanted me to have a normal life, and I'm sure they were worried that my wheelchair would get in the way of that. Plus, they knew Joe's family: his grandparents were farmers who lived in Swedesboro, where I lived. We even went to the same church and because Joe and I are only 2 months apart in age, we made our first Holy Communion together. Our families have pictures of Joe, Joann, and me from that day. I did not really know him then; we just happened to be in the same group of kids making their first communion that day.

My parents really liked Joe, but my dad was a little leery about our relationship, at first. Right after we met, Joe came over and wanted to take me to his house to meet his parents. I told him I couldn't go because Daddy was out working in the field, on the tractor, and I needed his permission to go anywhere. So Joe drove out into the field, to get my father's consent. That was before our first real date. And Joe and Daddy had a loooooong talk.

Daddy told him, "I trust you, but don't get into any hanky-panky." My father was especially protective because Joe was the first boy I went out with since my aneurysm. I had gone to school dances with boys, and I hung out on the boardwalk with boys, but Joe was my first real boyfriend. At one point while we were dating, my brother Julius warned me that Joe might break my heart, but I told him he was wrong: I knew Joe would not break my heart; I just knew. That went in one ear and out the other.

Our first date was the school homecoming dance. Joe had asked me to go out before then, but I kept putting it off because I was afraid to go on a date with him. Even though he was always so nice to me and so helpful, I was nervous because of my difficulty walking: I was worried that my disability would interfere with our relationship. I did not tell him I was nervous about my disability, but I guess he knew. And he was willing to be patient with me, until I was ready. Then Joann told me about the homecoming dance, and I really wanted to go, so that was my first real date with Joe.

Then, on the night of the homecoming dance, Joe was late picking me up. JoAnn's date was already at the house, and they were waiting for Joe to come, because they did not want to leave me and go to the dance and leave me home, in case Joe did not come at all. Also, many of my brothers and sisters were there because they were so excited for me: Julius, John, Rose, Grace, and Marie were there—in fact, I think all of my siblings except Linda were there, because Linda lived in Maryland at the time. So when Joe was late, everyone was getting worried that he wouldn't show up at all, that I would be stood up—which would have been especially embarrassing because Joann's date was there, and all my sisters and brothers were waiting with us for him to arrive.

After about 20 or 30 minutes, my mom brought me upstairs to my bedroom and had a long talk with me. She was trying to make me feel better, and she even offered to take me to the dance herself, which was sweet but not exactly the date I had in mind. I went back downstairs, still hoping he would come, and sure enough, a few minutes later, Joe knocked on the front door. I was all smiles, from ear to ear. But my Dad just looked at Joe and asked him outright, "Why are you late?" I did not care why: I was so excited that he was finally there. But he explained to everyone that he had gotten lost, and in 1989, there were no cell phones or GPSs, so it wasn't as easy as it is today to let someone know you're going to be late. He apologized, and I was so happy to be going to the dance with him.

I was all dressed up, in a black knee-length dress, and Joe was wearing a dark blue suit. He brought me a corsage of pink roses to pin on my dress, which looked so pretty. I had told Joe how much I loved to dance, before my accident, so when we got there, he took me out in the wheelchair on the dance floor. All the people around us were in awe, and my heart was pittering and pattering so much. I was very nervous when he took me out of the wheelchair to dance, because my legs get very stiff when I get nervous, and I did not want to embarrass him. But I could dance, with Joe's help. And that was magical. It was a magical night.

It was also magical because although Joe and I had been dating for about a month, we hadn't kissed yet. So I asked him that night, "How come you've never kissed me?" And that's when he gave me my first kiss, at the dance.

*   *   *   *   *

One time, Joe took me for a drive in his black Trans Am on a beautiful cool evening in May, and he saw how down and depressed I was on my face. He knew I was bothered about being in my condition and that all I wanted to do was to be able to walk again. So he stopped the car at a little park, on a somewhat busy road right down the street from his house. He did not say anything to me about why we had stopped there. Then he put on a CD, and the song was "You're my Inspiration," and it was really loud! He still did not say anything; he just got out of the car, came around to my side of the car, and then he helped me out of the car. I asked him, "Joe, what are you doing?" and he said, "Dance with me, Theresa." I said, "right here?" and he said, "Yes, I don't care who sees us or how you dance; I just want to hold you and show everybody who is in this park and driving down this road that you are mine. You're my inspiration, and I am so proud to have you, and I love you, Theresa!"

I'll always remember that breathtaking, captivating evening. He made me feel so exquisitely special, and the feeling in my heart was so strong that magical evening. It was like I was in a fairytale and I was being charmed by my striking, handsome prince, and my condition of being in a wheelchair did not matter to him. He loves me unconditionally, and he is so proud to have me by his side.

I knew I was going to marry Joe O'Connor, because my first crush was also named Joe. I was only in 8th grade when I liked the other Joe. He was a twin, too: he had an identical twin brother, Sam. We grew up together: his family were farmers, and my family were farmers. We rode the same bus together, and we always joked around and had fun on the bus. His sister Donna was also in my class. It was a coincidence that he and his twin knew me and my twin. In fact, my twin sister dated his twin brother, later, in the 10th grade.

I'll never forget the last day of 8th grade: it was June 8, 1984, and the other Joe had promised me he would kiss me after the graduation. I was so excited. I went to sleep the night before graduation, but my Grandmom died that same night, so I did not go to school the next day after all. That was a very sad day for me, for both reasons: I lost my grandmother, and I never shared a kiss with a boy who meant the world to me.

He did not have a crush on me; I just had a crush on him. We were friends after that, but our relationship was never the same, because we did not go to the same school anymore. He went to St.

James High School because he was two years ahead of me, while I was still at St. Joseph's Grammar School for another two years. I really liked him, though: I even wrote "Joe & Theresa" on a wall in the barn. I said to myself, *"I'm going to marry a man named Joe someday."* I can't describe how I knew this; I just knew. So when I met Joe O'Connor—that first day when he did the wheelies in my wheelchair—I immediately thought of the first Joe and how I knew then that I would marry someone named Joe. And I did!(But I'm getting ahead of my story again!)

I DID NOT WANT TO BE TREATED DIFFERENTLY

WHEN JOE AND I HAD been dating for a little over a year and a half, Joann had also been dating her boyfriend at the time for a while. One late evening during the summer, Joann was staying over at her boyfriend's house, but I had to come home. I did not understand why it was OK for Joann to be out and stay over at her boyfriend's house, but I wasn't allowed to. I was so angry with my Mom because she wasn't treating us fairly because of my condition.

So when Joe brought me home, I started to walk upstairs—and that was a big undertaking for me. When I opened the door to my bedroom, which I shared with Joann, I saw that the whole room was in shambles, which upset me even more. Just before I left to go out with Joe that day, I had made sure our bedroom was pristine—and that required a lot of effort for me to do. I found out later that Joann had left in a hurry, which is why the room was messy, but I did not know that at the time. I was so mad at my Mom and Joann and with my life, and I was just so frustrated with myself, my limitations, and my situation in general. I told my Mom how Joann left our room a mess, and I told my Mom that I did not think she was treating us fairly. I asked her why Joann was allowed to stay over at her boyfriend's house, but I wasn't allowed to. She gave me an absurd answer—so absurd that I don't even remember what she said.

I started crying hysterically; I couldn't even see straight. So I went to the bathroom, trying not to stumble and fall on the floor, and I looked in the medicine cabinet, and I found a full bottle of my mother's heart prescription pills. I was so tired with the world and with myself, and I felt that I would always be treated unfairly and differently from everyone else. I felt that nobody would ever see me as just me; they would see only my disability. I wasn't really angry with Mommy; I was just tired and fed up. So I swallowed the whole bottle of pills. I hadn't ever thought about suicide before, but I was so upset that I acted on impulse.

I heard Mom walking upstairs and finding me on the floor of my bedroom. She told me later that I was completely unresponsive. I was seeing everything double, and all I wanted to do was close my eyes and go to sleep. But I recall my mother's voice shaking as she frantically kept saying to me, "Theresa, stay awake! Don't fall asleep, hold on!"

The next thing I knew, I was in an ambulance going to the hospital, with my Mom right beside me, holding my hand, while the medics tried to pump out my stomach any which way they could. When I arrived at the hospital, I was still in and out of consciousness, and I still just wanted to be able to sleep. The doctors and nurses weren't very kind to me, and they had good reason, too. They gave me a chalky medication to swallow to subdue the rest of the prescription pills I had taken that they weren't able to pump out from my stomach.

The feeling I had afterwards was complete and utter embarrassment. I felt cowardly and ashamed of myself and ashamed that people knew what I had tried to do. The nurses made me realize that I had tried to take the easy way out, and they were right: taking those pills wasn't the right thing to do. After I was all settled and the doctors determined I was going to be OK, I decided that this was not the way to resolve my issues with my life and with my disability. I saw all the agony and fear in my Mom's face, for what I put her through. I also saw the tenacity in myself. I did a lot of soul-searching, and I made up my mind that I am not a quitter, and I was not ready to quit life yet. I'm here for a reason—everyone is here for a reason—and we just have to take life day by day.

So the hospital let me go home at 6:00 the next morning. When I got home, my Dad was waiting for me. My Mom and Dad put me to bed, so I would be able to get a couple hours of sleep.

When I woke up a few hours later and got out of bed, I unsteadily and very slowly walked downstairs. My Dad was sitting at the kitchen table, waiting for me. He told me to sit down beside him, which I did. He grabbed my hand and squeezed it real tight, and he said, "Holy Toledo, Theresa—I'll repeat my famous saying to you again—Holy Toledo!" Then, with a heavy sigh and a loving look in his eyes, he said to me, "Theresa, you know I love you. We all love you. There is a reason this happened to you. God chose you, out of all your brothers and sisters, because he knows you are the strongest of all them, and you can handle this. You can beat this, one way or the other. Theresa, I believe in you! Don't ever give up! Don't ever say you can't do anything you want to because you can make your life however you want it to be. So ALWAYS, HOLD ON! I'LL ALWAYS BE THERE FOR YOU; YOU'LL NEVER BE ALONE—don't ever forget that, kid!"

After he finished telling me all this, I held on to him, and I did not want to let him go. I told him, with tears in my eyes, "I'm scared, Daddy" and he said, with a shaky voice, "Don't be afraid, Theresa, you're stronger than you know, and if you do fall, don't give up. Have faith, Theresa: you'll find your way to pick yourself up again. I love you, kid, and I know you will conquer this!" All this time he was still hugging me, and he continued, "You hear me, Theresa? No matter what, don't ever, ever give up!!!"

Ever since my Dad spoke those words to me and whenever my life falls apart, and I think my dreams will always be unfulfilled and I won't be able to accomplish what I want to do, his words always strike a chord within me. I remember what he said that day, and his words make me even stronger yet. They give me the courage to never give up on myself and keep doing what was meant for me to do.

LEARNING TO DRIVE—
THE FIRST TIME

DURING THE 12ᵀᴴGRADE, A LOT of kids got their driver's license—in fact, some even got it in 11ᵗʰ grade. I was so torn up about this because Joann got her license, and my Mom bought her a car—a sporty Trans Am—and she could go wherever she wanted whenever she wanted. So one sunny Saturday morning, my brother Jimmy got the bright idea to let me drive his truck out in the field because he knew how badly I wanted to drive. I was so ecstatic and in such high spirits, because I actually thought I was going to be able to do this and drive his truck.

Jimmy drove us out in the field. We found a flat spot where I wanted to drive. He got out of the driver's seat and then helped me get behind the wheel. We got all settled and situated and then he asked me, "Do you think you can push the pedals with your feet?" I wanted this so badly in my heart that I overlooked the feeling that this could be a life-threatening situation (because I still had trouble moving my legs and feet.) So I just ignored what I was feeling and said, "yes."

Jimmy helped me put my legs and feet in the right position, where the gas pedal and brakes are. Then he tells me, "Theresa, when you start driving, just push slightly on the gas. And when you want to stop, don't slam on the brakes; instead, just push down on the brakes easy." I'll always remember what he said to me next: "Are you ready, kid?"I said, "Yes." He asked me, "Are you sure?"And I yelled, "yes!" So he said, "let's do it!"

That very instant, I scared Jimmy out of his mind because when I put my foot on the gas pedal, my spasticity kicked in, and my legs became stiff. Literally, my foot was pushing so hard on the gas pedal that Jimmy and I were speeding and zooming so fast in that field. Jimmy was screaming on the top of his lungs, "GET YOUR FOOT OFF THE GAS!" And I said, "Jimmy, I CAN'T!" He said, "HIT THE BRAKES!" And I said, "I'M TRYING!" Then Jimmy leaned over to the driver's side and tried to get my leg off the gas, yanking and pulling, and then finally he did. Then he put his foot on the brakes. We both looked at each other with shock and said with a frightening giggle, "We'll never do this again!" That's how scared and loony we were. I just really wanted to be able to drive, so I could be more independent, and Jimmy knew how much it meant to me.

Joe also knew how badly I wanted to drive, and he also thought I was capable of doing it. So one day after school, Joe picked me up at home and took me to an open parking lot. I asked him why were there, and he said, "I have a surprise for you: I rigged up hand controls for you, and the reason why we are here is for you to practice driving with your hands." My heart was racing with excitement, but on the other hand, I was a little hesitant because I did not want another episode of what had happened with my brother Jimmy!

Joe got me behind the wheel, and he explained how the hand controls work: "You push up for the gas, and you push down for the brake. You can do this, Theresa, I know you can." Joe told me to put the truck in drive, which I did. At first when I started driving, I wasn't too sure how to use the hand controls, and I was a little shaky with them, but with Joe coaxing me, it did not take me long to know how to use them.

I had been driving for a while in the empty parking lot when Joe told me that I did a really great job! Then he said, "Your next step is to go out on the road." I was a little uncertain that this was a good idea, but I knew Joe was right beside me, and I was confident that Joe would help me and prevent anything terrible from happening. So I said, "Let's go for it!" At first, I was being shilly shally about getting onto the road, but when I did, it was the greatest (but scariest) feeling in the world! I told Joe, "I can't believe I am doing this!" And he told me, "I knew you could drive; I never had any doubts you couldn't."

After I had been practicing driving on the road for a bit, all of a sudden, a big fat duck waddled out right in front of me! I put on the brakes and stopped right away. Joe was alarmed, and he asked me, "Why did you stop?" I said, "I did not want to hit the duck." He said, "Theresa, you slammed your brakes so fast and so hard that you could have gotten us killed if there had been a car in back of us! Another car would have hit us from behind, and they also could have gotten seriously hurt or even killed. Don't ever do that again!" I said OK, with assurance in my voice, because as I told Joe, "*That's not going to ever happen again.*"

But...I did learn a lesson from this situation, and my heart was tickled because the story did have a happy ending: I *DID* SAVE THE DUCK! YEAH!

Finally, the day came when I was supposed to take the driver's written test! Joe picked me up early that morning to go to the Motor Vehicle Department so I could take the test. I was raring to go and ready to take the written test, and I hoped I was going to pass and have my dream come true. Joe brought me into the building, and I got in place behind the computer to take the test. He gave me a kiss and wished me good luck, and then he waited in front of the building, hoping I was going to pass my test.

I did so well with the first 10 questions that I got excited. I thought my dream of driving would become a reality, and my life would become easier to do things and become more independent. But after the first ten questions on the test, I got stumped and baffled. I started to panic with fear, and my mind went blank, and I became unsure of which answer to choose. I still remember those moments of apprehension and worry that I was going to fail my test. My mind went to pieces with uneasiness. At the end of the test, I had such nervousness, because when I got to the very last question, I knew that if I got it right, I would pass the written driver's test. But if I got it wrong, I would fail the test. So I really concentrated, but I was so puzzled as to which answer to choose, and unfortunately, I found out later that I chose too many wrong answers.

After I failed the test, my dreams were crushed. I felt like a complete failure: it was a horrible let down, and I never wanted to put myself in the position of feeling that way ever again. As a result, I made up my mind and convinced myself that it wasn't meant for me to drive. So I stopped thinking I *was* capable of driving and instead decided I was *not* capable of driving. I stopped pursuing that dream, and I took the easy way out because I had Joe to rely on and take me places.

Thinking back on that decision now, I realize I fell short of so many things about what and where I could have been at that point in my life. My future could have been totally different if I had had a different attitude. Still, that was a learning lesson for me. It made me stronger yet because it made me realize I did not want to make that mistake again. I did not want to take the easy way out. I know now that everyone needs to be brave and overcome whatever obstacles are in your way, and try your best to reach your goals and dreams. Then you will never doubt yourself or wonder what you could have accomplished; you'll never think, *what could have been?* That's what happened to me: I still wonder *what could have been?*

MY SENIOR-CLASS TRIP

DURING THE END OF 12THGRADE, Joe and I were planning to go on our class trip together to Walt Disney World. But the School Board had so many issues about me going: they worried that I would slow down the rest of my classmates, that I wouldn't be able to handle the trip, and that I would require too much help. They were actually considering telling me that I couldn't go. I was fuming, and Joe was even more infuriated because he knew without a doubt that I could handle myself completely. Plus, if I did need help, he would surely be able to help me. It took a few months of convincing for the committee board to agree to let me go, but I felt there shouldn't have been any consideration at all about me not going!

When I did go on the class trip, it was so wonderful and grand. I wasn't any trouble at all, for anyone. I spent most of my time with Joe. I did not slow down my classmates at all. In fact, I was actually the first one on the bus in the morning, and I was the first one back on the bus at night to go back to the hotel. I did not get sick at all (the Board had been worried about that, too). Instead, two of my roommates at the Hotel in Walt Disney World got *sun poisoning!* What about that? I did feel bad for my roommates, but their situation also struck me as somewhat humorous. Then I thought maybe other kids got sick for a reason—to make the committee aware that they shouldn't have been so concerned about *me,* and they should have focused their energy elsewhere, on other problems that might (and did) arise!

I believe that I definitely shed light on what people with disabilities can do and made the School Board more aware of how wrong they were. However, Joe was right beside me. At the end of the class trip, my heart was so full of pride because it was such an incredible, outstanding trip, and I did not let my disability hold me back from anything I wanted to do (with Joe's help, of course!). Wow: what a great trip that was, in so many ways!!!

GRADUATING FROM HIGH SCHOOL AND GETTING MARRIED

AFTER WE CAME BACK FROM the class trip, the next big milestone in my life was high school graduation. I was *so* nervous when I went up to get my diploma. Joe was right beside me, because we graduated together. I was in my wheelchair, and when they said my name, Joe got me out of the wheelchair, and he walked up with me to get my diploma. There were thousands of people there, and when I walked across the stage, everybody clapped and stood up for me. I graduated from high school with a standing ovation as I walked up to get my diploma, holding on to Joe's arm. That was another very special day for me: I was so proud.

After we graduated, Joe and I went to vocational technical school for AutoCAD drafting. I went there for 3 years, and Joe went there for 2 years and was going to pursue it as a career, but there wasn't enough money in that career at that time, so he decided not to pursue it. Instead, he went to work for BP Oil Refinery, for about two or three years, then he worked for DuPont.

I really wanted to work with computers and do drafting. I won an award for a non-traditional career for women, for drafting. But after I graduated, I never pursued it because I wanted to get married to Joe. But I'm getting ahead of my story again!

*   *   *   *   *

A year after we graduated from high school and about three years after we started dating, Joe proposed to me, on March 24th—the date of my aneurysm. Joe thought that instead of this being a sad day, why not make it a happy, memorable one, so he took me to Atlantic City. I had no clue he was going to propose to me. It was a cold day, and we were on the boardwalk, when Joe brought me down to the beach, and I was *so* mad, because I did not want to go on the beach—it was too cold! I was in my wheelchair, and he helped me down the steps in it—which he always did, even on stairs and escalators in the mall: by this time, he had gotten very skilled at maneuvering my wheelchair. Still, I did not *want* to go on the beach. Then he got out a blanket and put it on the sand, and he took me out of the wheelchair. I did not say a word, because I was so angry with him.

Then he got down on one knee, pulled out the ring, and proposed to me. I couldn't breathe for a minute. I started to cry, but at the same time, I was smiling so hard my cheeks hurt. But I had to wait a few seconds to catch my breath before I could say anything. I felt like I was dreaming. It was the most incredible feeling in the world. Finally, I was able to breathe again, and I said *yes*. I was so happy.

Then Joe took me back to the Showboat Casino for dinner. I was smiling so much that everyone knew something was up with me. Also, I kept looking at my ring, so people kept coming up to me and asking me if I had just gotten engaged. I wanted to tell everyone that Joe had just proposed: it was such an incredible day.

People sometimes ask me if we talked about the fact that I'm in a wheelchair and probably will be for the rest of my life. But Joe doesn't see me in a wheelchair; he just sees *me*. He doesn't see me as a person who has trouble walking or who loses her balance and falls. He just sees me. To this day, though I worry about him sometimes, I know I don't need to, though, because I know Joe believes in me.

Joe has always been so attentive to me, from the very beginning, from the first day we met, when we were only 16 years old. He waited for me after school; he waited for me while I did therapy. He knows I'm the kind of person who will never give up, and one way or another. Joe believed in me more than I did. He knew we could get married and have a happy life together; he even knew we would have children. I worried about how I would be able to take care of a little one when I had difficulty taking care of myself. But Joe believed in me; he knew I could do it.

When we got home from the beach that night, Joe told his parents that we were engaged. His sister Danielle was also there and she was so excited for us, especially when she saw the ring he had given me. When I came home, told my parents, and showed them my ring, they were speechless. Both of them were so happy for us.

Once we started to plan the wedding, my mom was in her glory. *I* was in my glory! I had thirteen bridesmaids, and a little bride. Of course, Joann was my maid of honor, and I had girlfriends, cousins, and Joe's sister as one of my bridesmaids. Joe had thirteen ushers, including my brothers.

We got married a year and a half later, on September 25, 1993, at St. Joe's church (which is now called St. Clare's: it changed names a few years ago). More than 300 people attended our wedding, which also happened to be on Swedesboro Day, a big festival where everybody gets together, like the Italian festival of San Gennaro. That made our wedding day even more interesting. My brother Julius walked me down the aisle, and my father met me at the altar. I remember seeing him cry with his love for me in his eyes. Before I walked down the aisle, I saw my Mom walking to her seat, and she looked so proud and happy for me.

I wore a beautiful wedding gown, and Joe looked so handsome in his black tuxedo. He was all smiles. He was so skinny back then, just like his dad. Both our moms looked beautiful and very striking, too: they were wearing fuchsia pink dresses. I designed my wedding ring, using the skills I had learned in AutoCAD.

It was an amazing day. It rained, but people say when it rains on your wedding day, it's good luck. I had a flutter in my heart that day because I knew this was meant to be. I believed and had faith, and

I heard a whisper from within, that God had put Joe in my life to be my supporting and loving husband and to help me through my life's challenges. I just knew and felt it in my heart, and his parents were so supportive and caring towards me. They were always there for me, no matter what.

In fact, there are many interesting coincidences involving our parents: Joe's mom is named Teresa, and Joe's dad is named Joe—so there was already another couple named Teresa and Joe! Joe's grandmother is named Rose, and my mom is named Rose. Joe's mom's birthday is June 23rd, and my mom's birthday is June 23rd, but she celebrates it on the 24th because she was born seconds before midnight. My dad's birthday is March 20th, and Joe's birthday is March 19th. There were other "quinkie-dinks," too. This was God's plan. Joe and his parents are supposed to be here with me on my journey.

For our honeymoon, we went to Cancun, Mexico, for a week. The airline knew we were a newlywed couple, so they put us in first class; the airline gave us a bottle of champagne, too. It was a wonderful trip.

When we got back, we moved into our first house, which we had bought before we got married. It was in Clarksboro, New Jersey, which is only two miles north of Mickleton, where Joe grew up, and only about six miles from where I grew up, in Swedesboro. My brother Julius owned a few apartments, and Joe and I considered moving into one of those, but it just did not feel right when Joe and I went to see them. So Joe's mom took us to see this house near my Aunt Jenny, in Clarksboro. It was a two-story auburn shingle house. I wasn't worried about the two stories: after all, I had grown up in a two-story house, and one way or another, I was going to continue to climb stairs, although Joe carries me up most of the time. (I don't know what I'm going to do when I'm too heavy to carry: I always worry about my weight, for that reason alone!)

Anyway, Joe's mom and dad helped us with the down payment for the house, though of course we paid them back. We lived there from 1993 to 1996, when we moved to our current home, in Mickleton.

Our first house was right near my Aunt Jenny's house: the backyard of our house led to a farm field, and at the end of that field was Aunt Jenny's house. One day, I had this bright idea to walk over to my Aunt Jenny's. I was tired of being inside and cooped up in my house. Joe was at work, of course, and every day since we had gotten married, I had to rely on Joe to take me places after he got home from work. There were even some days I did not go out at all because Joe was too tired to go out.

So I decided to walk over to my Aunt Jenny's. I did not want to tell anyone I was going to take this hike, because I knew it would be a challenge for me. I just wanted to prove to myself that I could do it, I really wanted to be able to do it, and I did not want anyone to think I was being foolish or crazy. Plus, I wanted to surprise my Aunt Jenny with what I could do.

I started walking in my backyard, and when I reached the end of it, there was a big obstacle confronting me that I needed to cross in order to get to the field leading to Aunt Jenny's house. It was a *huge* hill!

I did not even know it was there. So I stood there for a few minutes with my walker, I thought about how I was going to get over this hill, and I said to myself, *you can do this! Don't give up now! Just take it slow and easy, watch out for any holes, and concentrate on your balance.* So I started walking up the hill, I started to become unsteady with my walker, and the first thought that came into my head was, *I should have told somebody I was doing this. I should have called my girlfriend Elena, because I knew what a great and special friend she is to me and she would help me out any which way she could. Plus, I knew she was home from work. So, if I do fall, someone would know my whereabouts because I could be on the ground for hours until Joe comes home.*

Fortunately, without my knowing it, my next-door neighbor was watching me the whole time. He was also in a wheelchair, because he was a paraplegic. Joe told me later that he saw me walking with the walker, and he saw how much difficulty I was having trying to get up that hill, so he kept watching me to make sure I was OK. The next thought that came to me was, *I can't back out now. I am not going to fall. I am going to get to my Aunt Jenny's one way or another. I can do this!!!!* I kept repeating to myself, *I can do this – I can do this!!!* There were a few times I thought I was going to fall, but I believed! I knew God was with me, and I had faith that He would keep me from falling down and that I would reach my goal of what I set out to do! Going up that hill was wearisome and frustrating for me, but I eventually did it, and I was so proud of myself: I kept saying, *Yes! Thank you God! Thank you God!*

After I reached the top of the hill, I had to think about how I was going to get through the next step of my journey, which involved walking through a pepper field. I did not realize until I got to the top of the hill that the field was planted with pepper plants! But that still did not discourage me or make me turn back because I had made up my mind: I was going to do this! So I started walking through the field, and with every step I took, I had to pick up my walker to move it because the walker's wheels couldn't roll through the pepper plants. It surely did take me a strenuous while just to get not even halfway through the field; meanwhile, I was getting hot and thirsty, and my wrists were starting to hurt from picking up the walker the whole time I was walking so far.

Then I started to become afraid because I felt I had been outside for hours (and I had no clue, of course, that my neighbor was still watching me walking in the fields). I suddenly realized that if I fell in this field, Joe would have no idea where I was when he came home and saw that I wasn't in our house. Then I wondered, *what if I do fall? How will I get up? What if no one finds me? I could be out here all night!* Then something came over me and I had a rush of chills.

Then my panic went away. I kept saying, *you'll make it.* I had this driven force of energy that nothing was going to stop me from reaching my goal, even though my wrists were in enormous pain, which was getting worse every time I picked up the walker.

When I finally reached the end of the field, and my aspiration was closer to my reaching it and completing my journey (and challenge), the feeling I experienced was electrifying excitement and appreciation for the difficult obstacles I had just overcome! I was proud of myself. And I realized that I had not done this alone: I thought to myself, *Thank you, God, forgiving me your help and strength. I am going to do this, with you guiding me!*

Then as I reached Aunt Jenny's driveway, I realized no one was home. I stood in the middle of her driveway for a few minutes, and then my wrists started to collapse. I saw people walking on the sidewalk, and I called for help, but nobody heard me. Finally, I couldn't hold on to my walker anymore: my wrists gave out, and I fell. There I was, sitting in the middle of my Aunt Jenny's driveway, where I would have to wait until someone came home—all because I wasn't able pick myself up from the ground.

Shortly after I was sitting there for a bit, my cousin Tony came home and saw me in the driveway. He was surprised to see me in his driveway, especially since I was sitting on the ground with my walker next to me, and it was obvious that I couldn't get up. He was also very *amused* by my predicament: he was laughing as he helped me up, and I had to laugh with him because I realized I must have looked pretty ridiculous sitting there.

Soon after he got me inside, Aunt Jenny came home and gave me all her attention and love. She was so proud of what I did, but she also told me, "Next time, Theresa, tell *someone* before you decide to take on an obstacle like that again!" I assured her that I would. She then asked me if was ready to walk back home! I smiled at the suggestion but told her I would wait for Joe to finish work and then call him to pick me up—to which she said, "I thought so, love!"

GOD TESTED ME— TO SEE HOW MUCH I COULD HANDLE

AS IF I DID NOT have enough to deal with already, with all the difficulty I had walking, I was also in not one but *two* car accidents—both in less than six months. The first one happened three months before we got married. Joe was driving (of course: I did not drive yet), and we were turning left, when another car came out of a side street and hit my side of the car. I hit the windshield—hard. I had to get stitches in the front of my head—about eight—and I was so worried I would have a bald spot on my wedding day, but they did not cut my hair. Today, though, I wish they had shaved my head there, because where the stitches are is a bald spot now: the hair never grew back. Luckily, Joe wasn't hurt, and the other driver wasn't hurt. I wasn't wearing my seatbelt, but after that accident, I always wore my seatbelt.

Well, I *almost* always wore my seat belt. After Joe and I got married, my friend Stacy also got married. Right before her wedding day, she had a bachelorette party, so my mom took me to get my hair done. I was so excited, I forgot to put my seat belt on. My mom was driving, and another driver failed to stop at a stop sign. The other car hit us so hard that our car went off the road and hit a building, a mechanic's garage (ironically). Our car was totaled.

I don't know what happened to the other driver, but I hit the windshield again, and my mom did, too. Actually, we hit each other at the same time, and my front tooth scarred my Mom's forehead. There was a bank next to the garage, and the tellers called 9-1-1, and an ambulance came. Joe's mom worked at a school nearby, and somehow she found out what had happened to us, and she came, too. I don't know how everyone got to us so quickly, but when I came to, it seemed that everybody was there.

I was in and out of consciousness, but I remember screaming. My mom couldn't breathe, and I was terrified that she was going to die. Another ambulance came, and they took us in separate ambulances to Underwood Hospital, in Woodbury NJ (about 7 miles from where we lived, in Clarksboro). The doctors wanted me to stay overnight, but all I wanted was to go home. My lip had split open, and my chin was cut pretty badly, and I had broken my right ankle. Even worse, my mom was in intensive care: she broke her ankle, she had a punctured lung, and she had broken ribs. No wonder she couldn't breathe.

The doctors put a cast on my leg, and they stitched up my face: I had about 20 stitches this time, and I had a big scar. A few hours later, I had plastic surgery on my face. The doctors were worried because I had hit my head pretty hard. But I was so insistent on not wanting to be in the hospital that the staff reluctantly agreed to my wishes and sent me home.

My mom was in intensive care for a great while; I don't remember how long. It could have been two weeks or several months. I don't know because I was so out of it. I had the cast on my leg for two months. I couldn't walk at all. I should have stayed in the hospital, but I wanted to go home. Joe's mom and dad were with me 24/7: they were incredible. I stayed at their house during the day, and they went above and beyond for me. It took about a week to find an aide, and Joe's parents and his cousin Cherie took care of me until the aides started. Cherie was a godsend: an angel from above! She really helped me out a lot, because Joe's parents had to work some days. Cherie really made me feel at ease and very comfortable. Then I had to have aides help me during the day, and Joe took care of me at night. I was only 21 years old, and I needed help doing everything, even going to the bathroom. I had aides come to our house for about six months or more.

I had trouble walking to begin with, so I couldn't believe this had happened to me. At first, I was so angry: after all, I had spent so much time in the hospital as a child, and then I had these two car accidents, one three months before our wedding, and the other three months after. I was also angry because of the scar on my face: how much more could I handle? I knew the scar would never go away. It's under my lip, all the way down my chin. I was so excited when Joe and I got married, just 2 months earlier. I was so happy to be married to Joe, and then the second car accident happened on November 19, 1993, so it was really hard for me to deal with.

But then I realized that this was *meant* to happen, and it happened for a reason. I thought God was testing me, but I realized God knows how much I can handle. That scar is still there today, but it's part of me now. I just accept it. I don't even see it anymore. For a long time, I was really self-conscious about it, but then I got over it, and I don't even see it anymore.

After the cast came off my leg, I had to go through physical therapy again, for about a year. My hands also started to curl up during this time, which made it difficult to hold things. I had more spasticity in my right hand. Now it's fine, but at the time, I was in a lot of pain and discomfort. I went to therapy in Woodbury. I had to do stretching exercises, to work out my ankle, on the stair machine. I went to therapy two days a week, and I had to go by taxi, because there wasn't anyone who could drive me. After all, my mom was in the hospital, Joe's parents were working, and my father was sick—he had been diagnosed with a brain tumor and wasn't doing well, so he couldn't help me at all.

Joe had to do everything for me: I couldn't drive, and because I was in a cast, I couldn't even walk! He did all the grocery shopping, all the errands, going to the bank, everything. He worked full time, then he came home. Before the accident, I made beautiful dinners, and I baked. But after the accident, I was stuck on the couch, and Joe came home and cooked.

While I was recuperating, I watched lots of TV and held my cat Lucky. He was my world back then. He was my first baby. Joe had found him before we got married: he heard a kitten crying, and Joe saw that he was stuck up a tree. So Joe got him down. Then the next day, he heard crying again, and the same kitten was stuck in the tree: he had climbed back up. So Joe got him down again, and this time, he called me and asked me if I wanted a kitten. He was pure black, and we named him Lucky because he was lucky that Joe rescued him.

Lucky and I shared such a bond of closeness, comfort, and unconditional love. Lucky always gave me unending kisses, cuddles, and laughs. He was a big and vital part of my life, and he helped me get through tough and rough days—and I had many of them over the years! Lucky was even in the car with me when I had my first car accident, in 1993. The police officers found Lucky and took him to the police station, and where Joe picked him up. He kept me company while my face and leg healed. He provided me with encouragement and strength to carry out daily living routines that most people take for granted. I needed Lucky as much as he needed me. I truly believe Lucky was here to help me through part of my life's journey, and I believe he knew it, too. We shared such an incredible and unbreakable bond that continues in my heart even after his death: he died at the age of 20, on January 28, 2010.

Lucky and I were so connected that the night Lucky passed away, I woke up from a dream where someone was telling me to get up. *It was this beautiful lady wearing a white flowing dress. She said, Theresa, Lucky needs you. Get up: he needs you; he wants you with him.* The dream was so vivid and so real: it really shook me up. I knew I needed to get up or I would regret it.

I managed to get myself out of bed and found my way to Lucky. He was lying on the floor, gasping for air. I went to him, tears falling from my eyes, and my heart was breaking more and more with every step. I kept petting him and saying, "I love you, Lucky; I'm here, Lucky, I'm here! I love you." Then I pressed on his belly softly to let him know I was with him. Suddenly, he lifted his head up, he looked straight at me with such a gaze and lovingly look in eyes. Then he gently put his head back down. Then and there, he passed away. From the moment of his passing, all I wanted to do was to embrace him and keep him with me forever. But Lucky knew I was going to be OK, and it was his time to let me go. All he wanted to do was not to leave without saying goodbye!

Then, to add insult to my injuries (literally), one of my aides stole from me. My shower gifts were in the basement: Joe and I hadn't even had time to put everything away when I was in the car accident with my mom. I was on the couch in the living room all day when the aides came to take care of me, so it wasn't until I was healed and could walk around the house again that I went downstairs and saw that quite a few of them were gone. The basement stairs were in the kitchen, and since I was in the living room, I couldn't see anything. I had noticed that this particular aide would step outside from time to time, but I did not think anything of it. After all, who would imagine that their aide would steal from someone she was taking care of, while I was lying down in another room?

By the time I discovered that some of my gifts were missing, the aide was already gone. I never got to confront her about it. I did not even file a police report, because it had happened several months earlier, and I did not have any proof. It was too late for me to do anything about it, so I just said, *let it go*. Her day will come someday.

All in all, I'm glad I realized that God was testing me. I learned that there's a mission and a purpose in my life: there's a reason all this happened to me. There's a light at the end of every dark tunnel. And I was going to continue to try to find it!

THE "MRS. NEW JERSEY" PAGEANT

WHILE I WAS STILL IN high school, one of my teachers suggested I enter a handicapped pageant. I thought to myself, *Why should I enter a handicapped pageant, when I'm normal just like anybody else? I shouldn't be labeled or judged or even categorized just because I am disabled.* Also, I believe genuine beauty comes from within, from what's inside you, not from your outer appearance, when you really think about it. So about a year after Joe and I were married, my sister Rose would come over my house on the weekends and help me clean my house. She would help me make my bed, vacuum, sweep the floor, etc. Whatever, I needed done she would help me with because she knew that I wasn't able to do it and she wanted to help me out as her sister the best she could. She would always tell me, Theresa, that's what sisters are for to help out each other and to get on each other's nerves (She was trying to be funny) She always went way above and beyond for me no matter what. That's why she is such an incredible sister to me! So one day she read in the newspaper that there was going to be a Mrs. New Jersey Pageant. She brought me the article describing it, and she really encouraged me to enter the contest. So I did! Rose made me realize I'm not going to let my physical limitations stop me from entering it because I am no different than any other girl.

The pageant was held in Long Branch, New Jersey, which is a beach town. It went on for three days, and it was a great experience. I was very nervous because I had to be on stage. Joe came on stage with me: the pageant committee allowed that, because I don't have enough strength in my arms to push my own wheelchair. So Joe pushed me on stage, and he helped me in and out of my chair. There was no talent portion of this pageant, just the questions.

The other girls were very nice, although a lot of them were shocked that I entered the pageant because I was in a wheelchair. A few of the girls were catty, because they were intent on winning. But the majority of the girls were very nice. I wasn't there to win the pageant; I did not even think I would make the top five. I just wanted to make a point. And I wanted to create awareness about people with disabilities, and show what life is really all about, to show able-bodied people that I could compete, too.

Out of the 300 girls who entered, 25 were selected as finalists. I was one of the 25, and I was the 4th runner-up! When I heard my name called, all I wanted to do was reach out to each and every one there and help them realize that it did not matter whether or not you have a disability: you can do anything if you try hard enough. Yes, we are all different, but we're also all the same in this world! What really matters is was what's inside one's heart. Success comes from strength and beauty comes from within.

JOE'S PARENTS WERE WONDERFUL TO ME

BEFORE JOE AND I GOT married and while we were engaged, I was at his parents' house one day, and as I was looking out of a window, a thought came to me, out of the blue. It was a whisper, a little voice that came to me and said, "one day, *you and Joe* are going to live next door to his Mom and Dad. "At the time, I just brushed it off because I thought it was a silly thought and something that would never happen. There had never been a "for-sale" sign in their neighbors' yard, so I never speculated that the house next door would ever go up for sale.

Then a little after two years after Joe and I got married, we found out that Joe's parents' neighbors were selling their house, for a really low price. Both of us were stunned! They did not even put it on the market; instead, they came to Joe and me right away because they knew the house we were living in was a two-story house, and if we bought their house, it would be so much easier for me to live in because it was a ranch-style house, all on one floor. Right away, we bought it!

When I found out they were selling their house, I remembered when we were first engaged, I had a thought that we were going to be neighbors with Joe's parents someday. I knew God had given me Joe's parents to help me throughout my hardship, and I praise my hands up to the Lord that I have them in my life as my second parents. I even call them Mom and Dad, as I do my own parents. Joe's parents are my silver lining in life. I know God is with me every step of the way, because *He* surrounded me with their love and help, with his tremendous glory. I knew, without thinking twice, that moving next door to my in-laws was supposed to happen. God was telling me this was where my soul belongs. This is where I stand in His presence, and I hold the key to open the door to my heart's home.

There were times I was in the darkness, but the thought of God always uplifted me because I always knew He was with me and would help me. I felt this way especially when I fell in our house, and I had to call Joe's mom at work to come pick me up off the floor. Fortunately, she worked right down the street from my house. Every time I called her, she always knew right away why I was calling, and in her concerned but caring voice, she said, "You fell, Theresa, didn't you?" and I said, "yes, Mom, I fell."And she always said, "I'll be right there." She rushed over as quickly as possible: it always seemed like she was right there, in an instant.

She also saw the worried and disturbed look on my face, because I hated having to call her at work to come and pick me up off the floor. She always tried to pep me up: she always told me(with a slight chuckle), "that is why you have me and Dad—to always pick you up off the floor!"But I could see how hard it was for her to pick me up. Sometimes, we debated with each other how she was going to get me off the floor, but she always said to me (though with a nervous laugh), "I can do this, Theresa, we'll figure out a way." somehow, she always managed to get me off the floor, no matter where I was.

Also, there was no one spot where I fell in the house: I fell in the kitchen, in the hall, on the bathroom floor, in the shower, even in the hallway closet once. The time when I fell in the closet, I loved the look on her face when she found me, and that made my situation so much easier for me to handle. Mom was trying to be funny and with her silly laugh, she said, "Theresa, are you hiding in the closet?" She made my embarrassing moment into a laughing moment of contentment. I had such a warm, loving feeling within me, towards her, and in my heart. I knew solidly right then and there, I am wrapped in so much love, and I am so lucky to have Joe's parents as part of my family.

Another funny time, I literally fell into the refrigerator, and I wasn't able to get out. Thank God, my walker—and everything that was in the walker's basket—fell out, too. What struck me as funniest was that the phone was right next to me inside the refrigerator. I knew and had a whisper from within that this was God's intent, because I knew if the phone had fallen anyplace else, I knew positively for sure that I wouldn't have been able to reach it: that's how stuck I was inside the refrigerator. So I managed to grab the phone and I called Joe's Mom and Dad, and they ran over in a split second. When they walked in the door, Dad said, "I'm here to rescue you, but Theresa, why are you in the refrigerator?" I said, "Because I fell in the refrigerator! Dad, get me out!" Meanwhile, Mom was trying to keep herself from laughing and chuckling.

Dad got me out in the twinkling of an eye. As soon as he did, I laughed at myself, too, because who could have ever imagined that I would fall into a refrigerator? Mom and Dad certainly never imagined that would happen. It was a funny moment for all of us.

Joe's Mom and Dad rescued me so many times after I fell, and knowing they were there for me helped set free a part of me: I wasn't as afraid because I knew they were there to help me survive my life's battle. God gave me them as my winning prize, as loving, dear, and valuable gifts to fuel the fire in my heart and keep me going.

MISSING THE FREEDOM TO
DO ANYTHING I WANT

CONSIDERING THAT I FALL OFTEN, I'm sure many people think I should just sit at home and find quiet ways to spend my time. But the aneurysm that burst in my head happened when I was only 14 years old, and it was very hard for me to miss out on more adventurous activities that other people take for granted. So when I was in my early twenties, my husband and I bought a pair of snowmobiles. Yes, snowmobiles.

Joe and I had no problem riding them the first year we got them. But the following year, in 1995, we had a very heavy snowstorm, and we were excited that there was so much snow on the ground and we could finally ride our snowmobiles again.

We called Joe's sister Danielle to see if she wanted to go riding with us. When she came over, Danielle and I decided to start riding while Joe was still shoveling the driveway. Danielle and I discussed whether we should ride in the field behind my house or on my street. We finally decided to ride on the road because there was still a large amount of snow on it, and it would be a lot smoother and easier to ride.

Before we left, Joe told me he wanted me to wear his thick, thermal, waterproof suit when I went snowmobiling. At the time, Joe was working for BP Oil Refinery: They provided what is called a survival suit that would keep you warm if you fell into the freezing cold river. I put on the snowsuit with Joe's help: it was huge and puffy, and I felt a like cross between the Pillsbury Dough Boy and the Abominable Snowman!

But when I walked outside (with Joe and Danielle's assistance), I was incredibly excited to be going riding on the snowmobile. However, every step I took was hard for me because my whole body felt so restricted in the snowsuit. When Joe realized this, he picked me up, carried me to the snowmobile, sat me down on it, and then helped me get my legs situated so I would be able to ride it. Then he started our snowmobiles and made sure they were OK to ride. Danielle and I put on our helmets, and off we went!

Riding down the road at a speed of 25 miles per hour was so thrilling. I actually had adrenaline running through my body. It just felt so right to have control of this machine and where I wanted to go. After Danielle and I had ridden for a bit side by side, she decided to get in front of me and I trailed behind her. I noticed she was traveling way ahead of me, so I started to go faster because I wanted to catch up to her. I went up a slope in the road, but I hadn't seen that the road was icy, and all of a sudden, I lost control of my snowmobile! It flew up in the air, I immediately fell off it, and the snowmobile and I both landed on our sides in the middle of the road.

It happened so quick, in a split second, that I thought it wasn't real: one minute I was on the snowmobile, and the next, I was lying in the middle of the road, not being able to get up. Fortunately, when I fell off the snowmobile, I did not feel a thing because I had on the puffy, well-insulated waterproof suit to keep me warm, and I also had a helmet to keep my head safe.

While I was lying on the ground, I was yelling for Danielle to come help me. I was very anxious and scared, yet I kept thinking to myself *Danielle, look back, turn around and look back!* And I kept trying to scream at the top of my lungs to get her attention. All I wanted her to do was notice that I wasn't behind her so she would see me lying in the road.

Then I looked behind me and saw a pickup truck coming straight towards me on the icy road. Then I *really* panicked, because it was unfathomable to me how I was going to be able to get up. My heart was beating and pounding so fast because I was literally stuck: I wasn't able to move at all, the truck was getting closer and closer, and the adrenalin was *really* pumping through me now. I looked up the road to see where Danielle was, when suddenly, I saw her getting off her snowmobile, running toward me as fast as she could, waving her arms back and forth for the truck to stop, and yelling "Theresa, Theresa, Theresa, oh, my Gosh!"

I twisted my head again to see how far away the truck was, and I saw it coming straight towards me. I thought the truck was going to hit me because it looked like it was going to slide because of the condition of the slippery, icy road. I closed my eyes and concentrated my mind and heart on Danielle's voice calling my name as she ran towards me. I felt she was giving me faith, and I felt someone telling me everything was going to be OK. I held to my faith, and when I looked up, the truck had stopped just inches away from me.

When Danielle finally reached me, she was completely out of breath. She saw I was OK because I was all smiles from cheek to cheek. I actually started laughing because I was so happy to see her and to feel the energy of being so loved by her. I said to her jokingly, "Danielle, what took you so long? I could have been killed! But I do love you!" She laughed and said, "You drive me crazy, Theresa! Don't ever do that again! I love you, too!" Then she bent down, and we both gave each other the biggest hug ever! She and the truck driver helped me get up and back on the snowmobile, and we made our way—slowly—back to Joe. I loved the feeling of independence riding on the snowmobile, but I know I need to be more careful.

DON'T FEEL SORRY FOR ME

WHEN JOE AND I WERE first married, it seemed that people who did not know about disabilities would judge my situation right away. Many times when we were out shopping or in a restaurant, and if Joe was pushing me in the wheelchair, or if I was holding on to Joe's arm to walk, they somehow assumed that I couldn't speak for myself. So they would talk to Joe for me. They actually thought I did not have my senses! That would make me so mad! Whenever this occurred, I wanted to give them a piece of my mind, and Joe would have to calm me down. But I still felt belittled, and all I wanted to do was hide. It would bother me for a bit, then eventually, I let it go.

I still clearly remember one time this happened. Joe and I were walking out of a restaurant, and I was holding onto his arm. A middle-aged lady came up to Joe and me, and she said to Joe, "I am so sorry your wife is crippled." Both of us were shocked to hear those words come out of her mouth. Joe looked at me, and I said to her, "Excuse me. You feel sorry for *me*? I don't think so. I feel sorry for *you*." I wanted to cry, but I did not because I refused to give her the satisfaction of seeing how much she had upset me. I was so proud of myself, because I kept my composure, said what I wanted to say, and I walked proudly out the door. Perhaps she got the hint and realized that wasn't the right thing to do or to say. No one should automatically judge or assume about others. There were many more occurrences after that, but that one was the most challenging! I don't care or need to remember the rest. So I let them go from my heart.

Another time, Joe and I went out for breakfast with my girlfriend Shanna one morning. I was holding onto Joe's arm, and we sat down in the booth. Then a man came up to me and said, "do you know how lucky you are to have a husband like that?"And I said, "yes, I do know how lucky I am. But he's lucky to have me, too." This was a complete stranger. What gives this guy the right? He doesn't know what our lives are like, what our marriage is like. He was just feeling sorry for me. I know I'm blessed. However, Joe's lucky, too: we're in this together, as a married couple.

Sometime has passed since those incidents happened to me, and what comes to mind as I think back on that conversation is another conversation I had with my brother Julius. Joe and I always went to breakfast with my Brother-in-law Johnny and Julius on Sundays, and one Sunday, Julius said something to me that I've never ever forgotten. I was telling him about how I fell while walking with my walker, and I was so scared and so upset and so frustrated. Julius reminded me, "Even God fell when He was carrying the cross. You just have to pick yourself up and keep walking until you reach whatever goal you want to reach, and never give up. That's what God did! Theresa, you can't be weak or weary. We all have a cross to carry—and some are heavier than others." When my brother said that to me, I was so stunned because he made me take hold of the concept and understand that God did carry His cross, and that each and every one of us has our own cross to carry. It's up to us how far we want to carry our cross.

I WANTED TO GO TO WORK

ABOUT A YEAR LATER AFTER Joe and I moved next door to my in-laws, I started to feel unfulfilled inside. I wanted and needed to do more with my life. I did not want my disability to hold me back from living a normal life. So I decided to work at A. I. DuPont Children's Hospital in Wilmington because it felt so right to help others that need help. I started volunteering in the Medical Records department, and I really enjoyed it.

Joe drove me back and forth to work. I volunteered three or four days a week. Joe drove me: we got up at about 4:00 in the morning. We went to breakfast before going to work, at a diner in Wilmington, right near the hospital. He dropped me off, and then he went to his own work.

I worked a full day: I got there about 6, and I worked until 4:00, then Joe would pick me up on his way home from work. Back then, Joe drove me any place I wanted or needed to go. I was very dependent on Joe during that time of my life. I did not think I was capable of doing things that would make me more independent and less needy. Little did I know what I would be able to do in only a few more years, but I'm getting ahead of my story again.

After I had been volunteering for about a year and a half, a thought came to mind. I realize now that it was a whisper from within telling me, *"Don't be afraid, talk to the president of the hospital, and ask for his help! If you don't try, then you'll never know. Give it a shot!* – I listened to my inner voice and I did. I asked the president if he could help me get a paying job in the hospital. I told him that

I felt I was capable and ready to be committed to a job and a place where my heart belongs; I felt in my heart of hearts that working at this children's hospital was where I was supposed to be. I wanted to help out in every way I could in the hospital and so on........ The president answered my prayers and made my dream come true: he helped me get a job in the Hospital Billing department! It meant so much to me that he believed in me and had faith in me: that was the ultimate vote of confidence, and his help motivated and encouraged me to do my very best at my job, because I wanted him to be proud of me.

I worked in the Hospital Billing department for almost eight years, and I absolutely loved it. All my coworkers were outstanding, and we worked very well as a group. Then, in the eighth year I was there, I had my daughter Samantha. As a new mother and with my disability, I found caring for her to be very strenuous, and I did not know how to overcome the hurdles that were in my way to take care of my baby girl in the best way possible. I decided to leave my job so I could focus my attention on my baby.

At times, taking care of her was so difficult and very challenging, but I stayed focused because I believed with all my heart that I could do this. I was not going to let my disability stop me or hold me back from doing the best I could for my child. I was blessed that God gave me the wisdom, the will, and the strength to be *the best mom I can be!* But I'm getting ahead of my story again, and before I could experience the joy of becoming a mother, I suffered the grief of losing a parent.

DEALING WITH MY FATHER'S DEATH

MY FATHER STARTED TO BECOME ill when he was about 60 years old and I was about 20. Over the next 10 years or so, he declined steadily. He had a tumor in his brain, and he started showing signs of either dementia or Alzheimer's. He seemed to get worse every day. Finally, one day when I was working at A.I. DuPont, my sister Linda called me and told me I should get to Underwood Hospital right away to see Daddy. I wasn't able to drive then, so Linda picked me up from work to take me to the hospital.

When I walked in his room, I did not expect to see what I saw before my eyes. Daddy was lying in his bed, in what seemed to be a frozen state: he wasn't able to communicate at all. My heart dropped with a terrifying feeling of emptiness. All I wanted was for my Daddy to be how he used to be. My heart was wrestling with the fact that my Daddy was going to die, and all I could do was put my arms around him real tight and keep telling him, "I love you, Daddy, I love you, hold on, don't give up!" just as he had said to me so many times over the years.

I also talked to him, trying to help him remember the fun times we had on the farm: "Remember how you would yell at me and Joann for bringing cats inside the house, so we would hide them? You found one in the bathroom hamper, and you were so mad at us, but you still had a smile on your face. Remember the time you took me and Joann crabbing at the shore, and we caught fish instead? What about every time we took a road trip to go someplace far, and we always stopped on the side of the road for lunch, and we always ate pepperoni and bread? Come on, Daddy wake up – wake up, Please, wake up, Daddy!" My heart was aching with so much grief, and big puddles of tears were streaming from my eyes. I thrashed about on his unmoving body, and I squeezed him as tightly as I could, with my head on his chest. At that very moment, I realized that Daddy had made me who I am, and I needed to be strong for him.

Then my Mom walked in, and then my Aunt Joe and Uncle Victor came into the room, and they asked me how Daddy was doing. I said nothing to them because I wanted to keep my composure. Then I said to my Mom, "He's going to die, isn't he, Mommy?" She put her arm around me, trying to be strong for me, and holding back her tears. But she said, "It seems to look that way, Doll!" Right then and there, I totally fell apart and gushed and cried every tear that was inside me. I grabbed onto my mom, holding her in my arms and saying *NO! NO!NO!* Then my Uncle Victor said "Tony doesn't even have a cross in his room, no rosaries, nothing!" I still remember the look on my uncle's face when he said that: it was a disturbing look of disgust, but I did not get upset with him at that traumatic moment because he was obviously distressed by the fact that there were no religious icons in the room. I knew that was a sign from the angels above for me to regain my self-control and go downstairs to the gift shop right away and get Daddy some rosaries and a cross.

So I rushed as fast as I could in my wheelchair downstairs to the gift shop. I went into the shop, and I saw a beautiful cross and several stunning blue-crystal rosaries, and I knew they were the ones for Daddy. So I bought them, and the sales lady put them in the bag, and I held them close to me until I got upstairs to my Dad. When I went into his room, I gave the cross to my Mom, and she put it on his bedside. Then I took out the rosaries and I wrapped them around his hand, hoping he would feel them and that I was there. I stayed for a while longer, hoping he was miraculously going to wake up. Then Joe came and he stayed awhile with me, until finally we both decided to go home to get a quick bite to eat, and then we would come back afterwards.

While we were cooking dinner, I was sitting at the picnic table outside on the deck, when the telephone rang. Joe ran to get the telephone, and when he answered it, an eerie, spine-chilling feeling that came over me. I just knew my Daddy had passed away. When Joe walked back outside, I saw the look on his face: he was disoriented and at a loss for words. Right then and there, my stomach dropped, and I kept shaking my head back and forth screaming, "NOOOOO, NOOOOO, NOOOOO!!!" Joe got me up from my chair and held me really tight and he said, "Daddy's dead!" Crying hysterically, I said, "Daddy is *not* dead." But Joe said again, "Daddy's dead." And again, I said, "that can't be, NOOOOOOOO…NOOOOOOO!" He shook me to help me regain my senses, and then he said again, "Theresa, Daddy's dead."

I wrapped my arms around Joe, and I was crying so profusely outside on my deck that my in-laws heard me, and they rushed over to see what was wrong. They saw how frantically upset I was, and they tried to console me. Then Joe and I rushed to the hospital to spend the last moments with my Dad before he was taken away.

When I arrived at the hospital and saw my Daddy dead in his bed, I felt as though my heart had been completely trampled. I got out of my wheelchair and I stood over his bed, grabbing onto his cold hand. Then I leaned down, holding onto his cold body, shaking him, never wanting to let him go, and I screamed, "Daddy, wake up, come back to us! Daddy, come back to me, I need you, Daddy! Wake up!" I continued to wail and yell at the top of my lungs, and I did not care who heard me. All I wanted was for my Daddy to wake up. But my Daddy died, on July 1, 2002: he was only 72 years old

It was hard to accept the reality that my Dad was gone, and I really had to restrain myself and keep myself under control to not break down during my Dad's funeral. I went up to my Dad's casket, and I felt so afflicted with so much distress and sadness. My heart was ripping out, but I managed somehow to find the power to have a hold over myself to get through it. When I looked at my Dad in the casket, though, I saw that he was free and at peace, with no more pain. I also saw that he had the rosaries I had gotten him, wrapped so beautifully around his hands. I just knew—because of a whisper from within—that Daddy had angels singing around him and that he was in a better place. The feeling I had was unexplainable, but it was entwined with so much incredible assurance. Overall, I knew Daddy's spirit was bringing us together: he was helping me come to terms with the idea and helping me to understand that he would always be with me and that I would never be alone. He'll always be alive in my heart!

My Dad and Buttons

My Mother, JoAnn and I a few months
before my aneurysm burst

Jimmy helping me walk by myself on the farm

Joe and Theresa 1992

Theresa's Family

My Father and I on my Wedding Day

My Mother and Father on my Wedding Day

Our Wedding Picture

Joe's Parents – (Mom and Dad)

Joe is helping me walk after our Wedding Ceremony

My Twin sister JoAnn with me on my Wedding Day

Mrs. New Jersey Pageant

Joe is pushing me on stage at the Mrs. NJ Pageant

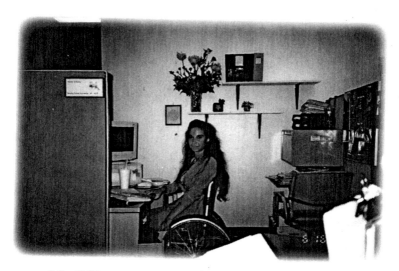

My Office at A. I. Dupont ~ Nemours Hospital

I was Guest Speaker at Nemours Hospital
for Disability Awareness

Did a runway show at Adelphia's Bar
and Grill in Deptford, NJ

My Baby Shower

10/10/2004

Two months after my Daughter Samantha was born

04/18/2005

Samantha's first trip

Going in the Ocean with Samantha at Ocean City, NJ

Taking Samantha to the park on my scooter

Samantha is helping me walk on the beach in Ocean City, NJ

Samantha and I playing air hockey in Ocean City, NJ

Samantha and I walking on the Beach together

Samantha is so excited I got on this ride with her!

Pulling Samantha on her tricycle in Ocean City, NJ boardwalk

Our Family Picture with my cat Lucky

Taking Samantha for a ride on her sled

Pulling Samantha on her sled

WEEE ~ we took a sled ride together

My Van with my Precious Samantha

Samantha being cutesy!

Samantha with her Mom Mom and Pop Pop

Disney World with Joe's Parents (Mom and Dad)

Disney World!

My Mother with her Grandchildren

Samantha and Mom-Mom
(My Mother) 80th Birthday Party

My Mother is my Sparkling Star!

HAVING A CHILD

ON AUGUST 1, 2004, MY whole attitude and outlook on life changed: Joe and I had a beautiful baby girl! My doctors had told us that it wouldn't be a good idea for me to get pregnant because of my disability, and they weren't too sure whether or not I would even be able to carry a baby to term. They said I would probably be in bed during most of the pregnancy. Joe and I were fuming up a storm: we were shocked that they actually told us we shouldn't try to have children! So we tried in spite of what they told us, and it did not take us very long to get pregnant. When I first found out, I was scared and worried because I did not know what to expect. I thought, *It's so hard just taking care of* me. *How am I going to take care of a little one?*

The first trimester was the hardest. I wasn't able to walk at all, and I had bad headaches. I slept all day. Joe had to carry me from place to place inside the house. I was so weak and sick that I had to go to Thomas Jefferson Hospital in Philadelphia for two weeks, and then I went to Magee hospital for a week for rehabilitation. But during that time, while I was in the hospital for rehab, I felt a flutter in my heart and a whisper from within—just like I felt when I got married to Joe. I just knew this baby was meant to be. My heart was telling me to get my priorities straight and to do my best, to go above and beyond what everyone else thought I was capable of, and to have a healthy pregnancy and a healthy baby. This was God's plan for me. So I gave all my worries and stress to God. I believed and had faith that God would give me the will and the strength to be strong, and that my physical limitations wouldn't stop me from being the best mother I could be.

During my pregnancy, my really close and beautiful friend Elina helped me a lot. She got pregnant two months before I did. The funniest thing is that we didn't even talk or discuss about thinking or trying to get pregnant. So, when she found out she was pregnant, it was hush - hush to everyone. She wanted to make sure everything with her pregnancy was fine before she announced to everyone the happy news, including me. When I called her and told her I was pregnant, she was screaming so loud that she was actually hyperventilating over the phone. In fact, Joe could hear her and he was sitting across the kitchen table. I could not figure out why she was screaming so loud until she finally calmed down. That is when she told me she was pregnant too. Now I was so ecstatic and over come with joy. I just knew from the heaven up above that this was God's plan and we are suppose to share our lives together as really special friends and our children as well. The remarkable thing is she has Beautiful Twin Girls!

I worked out every single day, one to three hours a day, mostly doing leg presses and my stair machine at home. I went to work three days a week. I tried to keep myself active and moving, and I took cat naps when I needed to. I ate very healthfully (though I did splurge with ice cream twice a week!). I was determined to prove those doctors wrong! Just because I was disabled did not mean I couldn't have a healthy pregnancy and a healthy baby. On August 1st, 2004, I had a beautiful baby girl, and we named her Samantha Lynn O'Connor. God gave us the most precious gift of all! After I had my daughter, I became aware of so many things I needed to do in this lifetime to be the best mother I could be, just like my mother had done for me when I was a child.

At first it was so hard. I needed help taking care of her because I couldn't even carry her from place to place. All I wanted to do was be with her, to be her mother; she was my responsibility. I did not want anyone else to take care of her, even though it was hard on me. But I had to rely on other people, because I did not have the physical mobility and strength to take care of her alone.

I hired someone to help me during the week, but she did not stay long. We got into an argument one day when she was taking Samantha out of the crib: she thought I was giving her attitude, but I was just frustrated that I couldn't do it myself. So she just walked out on me: she literally left the house, with Samantha crying in the crib. And she never came back. I was stunned, but somehow, I held on to the crib, and I held on to my walker, and I got Samantha out of the crib. I held her really tightly and was able to get back to my chair, where I sat down and held her until Joe came home about an hour later. That was a difficult day, but we were fortunate to find other, more reliable people to help me over the next few years until Samantha went to preschool.

The next person I hired to help me after my beautiful baby girl Samantha was born was Joe's cousin Linda, who has two children of her own. Actually, Linda is married to Joe's cousin Frank, who looks somewhat like my husband (not surprisingly, since they are first cousins). Linda is in her late thirties, and she's very slim and tall with a thin oval face and short blond hair. Her energy and spirit are so alive and enthusiastic, and she has a positive aura that is so feisty and strong. It actually gave my heart so much more driven zest and fire to be the best mother I could be and to overcome any hurdle and obstacle that was in my way, to take care of my daughter to the best of my ability.

Linda helped me find my way to becoming a mother. She made a great impact on me by showing me how to take care of my daughter, by helping me clean the house, and by being a sweet and loving cousin and beautiful friend. She was such a tremendous and incredible help to me in so many ways. There were many sleepless nights when I lay in bed, trying to figure out ways to deal with my disability. My heart was aching because I was so afraid and worried about how I would be able to take care of my little one if Linda couldn't help me. I knew deep within, though, that Linda would try her hardest to be there for Samantha and me. She reassured me often, and when I couldn't sleep, I would think of her telling me, "Theresa, there's no need for you to worry. I will be there to help you take care of Samantha and with everything else. Trust me!" Eventually, I would drift back to sleep, with her words in my dreams.

Linda, if you read this, I want you to know that you are an outstanding person and cousin. When I was a new mother, you made me feel so much more at ease with my disability, and you helped me become a nurturing and loving mother. *Thank you!*

Even with Linda's help, however, Samantha's first few years were very tough on me emotionally, because I did not want my physical limitations to hold me back any longer. I really wanted to take care of my daughter. I felt very strongly in my heart that I was her mother and that she was my responsibility. My whole approach to life changed. I asked God to help me figure out a way to do the things I needed to do. I wanted God to take my hand and lead me in the right direction. I wanted that closeness, that bond, that quality time that a mother and daughter should have. I just wanted to be able to take her places, instead of relying on other people to take us. And God showed me the way.

A few weeks later, my mother asked me if I wanted her scooter. I hadn't even considered this before, and she hadn't mentioned it before because she did not think I would be able to ride it. But one day, she realized it should be my decision. When she suggested it, I had a whisper from within and realized the scooter could be a new beginning for me, because I would be able to do things alone with my daughter! Samantha was about a year old then, so she could sit on my lap on the scooter, so I started taking her to the park, to the library, and all around the neighborhood. It was the greatest feeling in the world just to be able to take her places alone. I felt this was the start of a more independent Theresa.

But I did have a few challenges taking my daughter around on my scooter. One time, we were riding the scooter over a railroad track and we got stuck. My scooter wouldn't budge. Samantha was about two at the time. I tried to move the scooter, but I wasn't able to move it because I can't walk without my walker. I did not know what to do, and Samantha was sitting on my lap. I have never been so scared in my life because there were two vehicles coming towards us in different directions! I felt totally helpless. I wasn't sure whether to take my daughter off my lap and tell her to run, or would that make matters worse? I was afraid that a car or truck on the road wouldn't be able to see her and they would hit her. So I made a split-second decision and I just prayed to God that they would see us. I waved at the trucks that were coming towards us in different directions. They stopped and helped us get my scooter off the railroad tracks. THANK YOU, GOD!!

Fortunately, the railroad fixed the tracks after that incident, and I was even more careful than before about where I went. I wasn't going to give up riding the scooter, though, because I really wanted to be self-sufficient and independent.

When Samantha was about two years old, I started taking her to the park regularly. It was nice to be outside, in the fresh air, around other little kids, but sometimes being there was really hard for both of us. Still, we would try to make the best of our situation by ignoring what we couldn't do at the park and focus on what we could do. In fact, I couldn't even *put* her on the swing and get her off. That did break my heart terribly because that was one of the things Samantha wanted to do most. But I had to think positive and try to make Samantha still have a great time at the park. Therefore, we usually went during the week, when Joe was at work so Samantha and I could have Mommy-and-daughter time together. We still had a good time. There weren't very many things we could do at the park, but I would pack her a lunch or a snack, and we would eat it there, I read books to her and played games with her. I made the best of it.

Joe and I wanted to have more kids, but our main priority was Samantha. We feel very blessed and fortunate to have her. Ever since she was a baby, it seems she sensed what I could and couldn't do, and she made allowances for that. For example, she never ran away from me; she never left my side: she just seemed to know that she wasn't supposed to wander off, as most children do. She knew she needed to stay near me. She seemed almost *protective* of me, even when she was really little.

Samantha really tickles my heart because of how she understands my position of being her disabled mother. I know without a doubt that she knew from the very beginning, from the day she was born, about how I wasn't able to carry her from place to place. I remember that point in my life of being her mother was a very crucial time for me because it was so hard when Samantha cried or was cranky, or when she wanted to be fed, and I needed help from someone who could pick her up and to place her in my arms or wherever she needed to be.

Samantha has tried to help me even when she was just a toddler. The day after Christmas one year, when Samantha was only two years old, Joe went to work and Samantha and I were home alone. I had this bright idea to look through the gifts that were under the Christmas tree. I knew I had to be very careful because of my balance. With every step I took, I had to maneuver my walker very slowly. I was especially unsteady because all the gifts were in the way. In spite of how careful I was, I tumbled over on one of the gifts I wanted to look at. Somehow, my body twisted, and I landed on the floor with quite a few gifts on top of me!

There was no way I was going to be able to get up, but I was able to grab the phone from the basket that hangs on my walker. Meanwhile, my cat Lucky knew I was in pain, and he ran right to me after I fell, meowing loudly. I tried hard to move my legs to a position where I would have some leeway and be able to move some of the boxes that were in my way, but that did not alleviate the pain that was running throughout my body. I just couldn't completely untwist my body. Lucky stayed by my side, and he put his head in my lap, letting me know he was with me.

I called Joe's mom and dad first, but they weren't home. So I called my Aunt Jenny and my cousin Tony. Tony answered the phone, and when I told him what happened, he rushed over right away. Unfortunately, Tony wasn't able to get into the house because all the doors were locked and the garage door was shut. While Tony was trying to figure a way to get into the house, Samantha was trying to move the gifts that were surrounding me and on top of me, so I would be able to try to position my body better and be more comfortable and in less pain while I was laying on the floor.

As Samantha was moving the gifts, Lucky was still by my side— until Tony broke the front window. Then Lucky ran up to the window while Tony was trying to climb through it. Meanwhile, Samantha did not know what was going on. Her eyes got so big and she looked frightened, so I tried to soothe her, telling her, "it's OK, sweets: it's cousin Tony. He's helping Mommy." While Tony was trying to squeeze through the window, he asked me, "Theresa, are you OK?" I said, "Yes, I'm hanging in there, Tony." Then Tony laughed and said, "Your cat doesn't want me to come through your window: he's watching me like a hawk. Theresa, your cat is like a watch dog!"

After Tony got through the window, he came over to me and helped me up off the floor. He stood me up and made sure I was OK and that there was no more pain. I took a few steps to the couch, sat down, and took a deep breath. Samantha ran right beside me, then Lucky ran over to me, jumped on my lap, and put his head on my thigh. Tony had a big smile on his face as he said, "Your cat is one very special cat. He is your protector and guardian."

I answered back, "I know he's very special. Samantha and Lucky are both my babies."

He chuckled and said, "You sure are well loved, Theresa." I know that's true—not only that day but every day. So I wrapped my arms around Samantha and Lucky and squeezed them real tight, and then I gave Tony a hug and thanked him for all his help and for being a *TERRIFIC* cousin. Just like the day he rescued me when I decided to walk across the fields behind my house, Tony came to my rescue again that day.

* * * * *

As Samantha started walking, it got easier for me to be more independent and take care of her, instead of having to rely on other people to help me. I knew in my heart that Samantha understood what my limitations were because I would take her to the park and there was a busy road next to the park and she never left my side. She would play around the park grounds; go on the wooden choo-choo train or the see-saw. I would play with her to the best of my ability, and we would have lunch. We went to the park 3 or 4 days a week, and she was always very well-behaved and listened when I said "NO" to something, whereas some toddlers at the age wouldn't have listened very well when their parents say NO. They run off from their parents and dash so fast from them that the parents often have trouble actually catching them.

One time, we were at the park, and I wasn't able to budge my scooter at all: it had gotten stuck. There was no-one around to help me. She was about 3 at the time, and she sat on my lap when I was on the scooter. So I had to put her down and get out of the scooter, and tried to push it out, standing and holding on to the side of my seat from where it was stuck. I don't know how I did that, and I couldn't believe she did not run away from me—because most kids would have run away. And it was such a busy road! God must have been watching over us, though, because Samantha never left my side. She just sensed that she needed to stay with me.

There have been lots of other challenging incidents and teaching moments in my life. Going to the library was particularly hard. I was able to take Samantha to the library on my scooter because it's only about a mile away from my house. But the library had steps leading up to the entrance, so I wasn't able to get in; also, the bathroom was in the basement. The library did have a wheelchair lift, but it was broken. At first, I was upset with the people on the library staff, because they hadn't fixed the wheelchair lift, and it had been broken for a while. I was also really angry and upset with myself, the world, and with God. *Why? Why me? Why can't I walk the way I used to walk?!!*I felt so broken and torn up inside because I saw other mothers walk into the library with their children, and I couldn't. My heart ached for Samantha. But I realized that was not going to stop me from going to the library with my daughter! She was not going to miss out just because of my disability. No way!!!

Once I had made up my mind that we were going to find a way into the library, I decided to drag my walker behind my scooter. Every time we went to the library, my walker came along with me. That is how I got into the library. The librarians were very nice and understanding. They carried the walker up the steps, and they helped me and my daughter. (Eventually, they did fixed the wheelchair ramp.)But some days, there were moments when I just wanted to cry because I saw my daughter waiting so patiently while I walked slowly up the library steps and I saw other mothers with their children walking so easily and quickly up those steps. But I just knew from deep within that I was and I am so blessed. I am thankful in so many ways. Samantha is my miraculous gift from God, and when she grows up, she'll know the importance of patience and caring and understanding for other people in all situations. I'm her prime example, and as her mother, I need to be strong because it is not about me anymore. It's about my daughter. All I want is for my daughter to love and to experience life to the fullest.

* * * * *

Another place that I had problems was at the beach in Ocean City, NJ. Before Samantha was born, Joe and I used to go to the beach during the summer months, and Joe had to carry me onto the beach because I did not think I had the strength and ability to walk, and I did not want people to think any differently of me. Plus, I also was afraid of falling. Thinking about it now, I realize I was being cowardly and I wanted the easy way out. So after we had Samantha and we went to the beach in Ocean City, New Jersey. I would bring my walker onto the beach and walk with my daughter Samantha. I'm proud of myself for doing this, and Samantha also gets excited when I set goals for myself and try to walk a few blocks onto the beach.

One summer day, on the beach in Ocean City, I made a bigger goal for myself, and I was so determined to reach that goal. I wanted to be able to walk five blocks, with my walker, on to the beach. It surely did take a while—a really long while. It was a hard victory, but I did achieve my goal. During the entire time I was walking, Joe and Samantha tried to occupy themselves: they played out in the ocean, they played Frisbee, they even went to the amusement park on the boardwalk. They did check up on me quite a few times to make sure I was ok and that I hadn't fallen. Quite a few people on the beach were cheering for me. Numerous people came up to me and asked me if I wanted any help or if they could get a chair for me to sit down and take a break and rest. But I told all of them, "I really appreciate you asking me if I need help. Thank you, but I need to do this on my own. I made a goal of wanting to walk 5 blocks, and I am going to do this, no matter what. I AM NOT GOING TO GIVE UP!"

During that 5-block hike, I had a few scares where I almost fell, but when I finally reached my goal, I was so ecstatic. I said to myself, *Oh my Gosh! I really did it. Thank you, God!!! Thank you!!! Thank you, God!!!* Samantha was jumping up and down. She was so extremely happy for her Mommy! Joe put his arms around me and said to me, "You know how much I love you, and you have to realize

I am so proud to have you as my wife. I knew you could do it. I had no doubt whatsoever! I believed in you and I know you will never give up until your goal is reached!!! You are not a quitter, Theresa!"

Then he said, "Now you have to walk back to our spot where we had our towels and things," and I said, "WHAT!!!" He was trying to be funny, of course. I did walk a bit on the way back to our place on the beach, but my sweet and loving husband carried me the rest of the way because he knew I was totally wiped out. Yes, it was so incredibly hard walking that whole entire distance, but I felt the greatest feeling of accomplishment in my heart that I had achieved this goal. I felt such potency and power because I had not given up. *I did it!!!!*

It's still hard for me to do some things, especially getting into buildings that have steps. Not too long ago, when Samantha was about 7 years old, I took her to a birthday party for one of her friends. All the other girls were there with their mothers, and I wanted to go in, too, but there was no way for me to get in the house, because there were steps, and they were very high. Samantha said to me, "That's OK, Mommy, I'll be OK by myself." She tried to make me feel better, but I still felt bad because I wanted to be there with her, but I just couldn't get in the house. She accepts my limitations even better than I do, and I appreciate that, but I still wish I could do more.

As Samantha has gotten older, she has become more aware of things I have trouble doing, like picking things off the floor, folding blankets, making her bed, putting dishes in the sink, sweeping the floor, and doing other everyday household work. To this day, she helps me so much and I don't even have to ask her: Samantha just does things for me. She is my Radiant Star! She is so incredibly astounding to me and when she grows up, she will also be aware and have the understanding that we're all the same but we're also different in this world. That each of us is no better or less than anybody else. We're all created equal!

Recently, Samantha noticed that I have trouble getting into her bed, which I do every night until she falls asleep. I couldn't lift my legs up on to her bed. So my sweet precious daughter asked me, "Mommy, do you need help putting your legs onto the bed?" I said, "Yes, sweets!" Samantha said, "Mommy, don't worry: I got your legs. You're not going to fall off the bed; I've got you." And as little as she is, she helped me put my legs onto the bed. Then I had trouble covering her up and myself with her blankets on the bed, so she did that, too: she covered both of us up, and we said our prayers. Then Samantha said, "I love you, Mommy, you're the best!" My heart melted like butter when she said this. Then she gave me a really big, squeezable hug, and we held each other really tightly, until she fell asleep.

I've told her I had a brain aneurysm that burst. She doesn't really know what that means, but she's very aware of what I can do and what I can't do, and it doesn't matter at all to her. When she was about 5 or 6, she saw a video of me dancing, before the aneurysm burst, and she shouted with delight, saying, "Mommy's dancing! Mommy, you're walking!" Joe did not even tell me he had this video. He must have gotten it from my family. Samantha just loved watching it, and I got a kick out of watching her enjoy it so much. Samantha is really amazing. She never gets frustrated because I can't do something. She doesn't want me to get upset; all she wants is for me to be happy. She's my Radiant star. I'm so blessed.

I tell Samantha how I feel about her because I know it's so hard for her to see other mothers do so many other things that her mommy can't do. I can't go into certain buildings or homes because they don't have ramps or because they have gravel in the driveway, which my scooter can't ride through. And I can't get into some stores because their aisles are too small to get through, or there are too many people in a store so my scooter won't fit.

One particularly frustrating and disturbing time, I wasn't able to get into a store with her because it did not have a way for me to get up the curb in my scooter. Another time, I took Samantha to her acting classes, and after she was done, we decided to take a ride through the town of Pitman on my scooter. Most of the stores did not have ramps, only steps, and it was so heart-wrenching and upsetting to me that I wasn't able to take Samantha into any of the stores. I remember thinking, *don't cry, Theresa, don't cry.*

I put on a strong face for Samantha, but my heart was breaking inside. I kept talking to her, saying encouraging words about my situation, trying to distract her from the fact that I couldn't get into these shops and putting on a happy face. I tried any way possible to view the situation in a more positive light. But my ultimate wish, deep down, was that I just wanted to be able to get out of this jail of a scooter and walk the way I used to walk and not be limited whatsoever. Seeing other parents with their children walking into these stores and being so free and able-bodied and not physically limited makes me want to scream my lungs out!

But Samantha always has a big smile on her face and tries not to show that the situation bothers her. She tries to be strong and brave because she doesn't want me to get upset. She doesn't want my heart to throb for her or for myself. All she wants is for her mommy to "be happy," which she's always telling me. And all I want for *her* is to be happy! Samantha definitely knows how to cheer me up and lift my spirits: she'll give me a really big hug around my neck at those difficult moments. She knows that will always bring the love I have for her in my heart and a big smile to my face. She says to me, "I don't care that we can't go in, Mommy. You're my Mommy: you're the best, and I love you!"

At times like those, my eyes fill with tears, and then all that negative energy and pain dissolves away, making me realize how extraordinary and special my daughter is and how *incredibly lucky* I am to have Samantha as my daughter! I know she is *my beautiful gift from God!* So I wrote her a letter recently, to tell her how I feel about her:

January 28, 2013
Dear Samantha,

What a precious gift you are to me: I am so blessed to have you as my daughter. It tickles my heart how much you changed my life when you were born and I became your mother. You made me see so many things that I wasn't aware of before and never imagined doing. You, my beautiful Samantha, made me find the power and strength within me to strive to be the best example for you as your mother because I love you so very much. Words can't even describe how much I love you!

So I want you to find and realize your own strength and power within yourself. If I can reach the unreachable, believe the word *impossible* is not a word, overcome and beat the hurdles and obstacles that confront me, and never give up. Then you'll also find that golden key to unlock the door to your own strength and capacity in your heart, and you'll be aware of what potency and power you have in your life, Sweets! If Mommy can do it and have faith to never give up, then you can do it, too!

Believe in yourself and focus on the positive not the negative. I know that is so hard to do sometimes, but I want those qualities embedded inside you, so you can rise above anything that's in your way, whatever is blocking or discouraging you from achieving your happiness, goals, and dreams. Believe and have faith, Samantha, and you can prevail in your life, however you want your life to be Beautiful! Never give up!!!

I Love You!
Mommy

FINALLY GETTING MY DRIVER'S LICENSE

WHEN I WAS 34 YEARS old, I decided to pursue getting my driver's license, with my niece Christine's help. She gave me that little push and I want to thank her for it! I was afraid to take the written test because I had taken it before, back when I was in high school, and I failed it, by only one question that was incorrect. That failure really tore my heart out, and ever since then, I was afraid to take it again because I did not want to fail again. But Christine made me realize that I would only be a complete failure if I *don't* try and do my very best! So she persuaded me to start studying the driver's manual again, which I hadn't done in years, not since I was 16.

Then one day, Christine came over to help me with Samantha, and out of the blue, she said, "Theresa, let's go down to the Motor Vehicle Department so you can take your written driver's test." I said, "No way! I AM NOT READY!" And she said, "Yes, you are, Theresa: you have been studying for months now, and you have this driver's manual down pat.I know you are ready! Don't be a coward; you'll never know if you can do it, if you don't try."

I really thought about what she said, and I realized I can't be afraid. I knew from a whisper from within me that getting my license would change my life completely and for the better, for me and for Samantha and Joe. I would have the independence I had been fighting for all these years. I also knew it would open up so many doors for me and broaden my horizons: so many things that were impossible before would be possible, if I could drive!

So Christine took me to take the test—and I passed, with flying colors. Christine, I want to let you know that you're incredibly special to me, and yes, you are my niece, but you are also my remarkable sister!!! I want to say, "Thank you!"

But a lot of people, including some of my family members, were negative about the idea of me driving. It hurt my heart immensely, because they should have known that I wouldn't put anybody at risk of injury. I knew what I could and couldn't do with my disability. But I did not get discouraged. I put the negative aside, and I stayed focused. As long as you have the will to believe in yourself, and have faith, and don't get discouraged, you can fulfill your dreams. I positively believed, deep in my heart, that someday my dream would come true and I would drive my very own vehicle. So I overcame the obstacles that were in my way and succeeded. My dream truly did come true!

*　*　*　*　*

Since I had passed the written driving test, I needed to learn how to drive, though I would have to have on specially outfitted vehicle for my disability. Joe made some calls to various rehab centers, to find someone who knew how to drive with hand controls and could teach me. And he found Lynne Mason, who is a really good driver, and she was a *tough* driving instructor. I did not have a car with hand controls yet (though I do now), so she came with her car, which did have hand controls. Lynne isn't disabled; she's an occupational therapist at Moss Rehab who specializes in teaching people how to drive with hand controls. She had been teaching for years already when I met her. The first day she came, I did not tell my parents or Joe's parents; I wanted them to be surprised.

It was so freeing for me, to get behind the wheel and drive—I was so happy, because I knew if I could learn to drive with the hand controls, then I would have another measure of independence. I wouldn't have to be dependent on Joe to take me everywhere, or on

Joe's parents, or on anyone. I would be able to drive myself wherever I needed to go! Most people take that for granted, but I sure did not! As much as I appreciated all the help I got from everyone in my life— my parents, my sisters and brothers, Joe's parents, and of course, my wonderful husband—I still wanted to be more independent. I also wanted to be more of a help for my daughter, so it was important for me to master this skill.

That's why I did not tell anyone I was taking lessons. And on that very first day, at the end of my first driving lesson, it was such a great feeling when I drove straight to Joe's parents' house, and I got out of the car and said, "Surprise! I'm driving!" I told them I had started taking lessons on a car with hand controls, and I introduced them to Lynne and told them how she was teaching me and helping me. And they were really happy for me—and very encouraging, too, which helped me a lot. I couldn't wait to call my mom, which I did later that night, to tell her that I was taking lessons. And she was so excited for me! Of course, I had driven this way once before, when Joe and I were teenagers. But I did not realize what the consequences could be back then; I could have killed myself. I did not know what to expect.

The hand controls are very simple: you pull up for the gas, and you push down for the brakes. And there's a ball on the steering wheel, which helps the driver get a better grip on the wheel, so I can turn it more easily than if I had to grasp the wheel with two hands, the way other drivers do. The ball works almost like a computer mouse does. In Lynne's car, the hand controls connect directly to the gas and brake pedals. Some cars have a brake pad to prevent the driver's feet from touching the brakes, but when I was learning how to drive, that wasn't there, so I had to be extra careful. I had to push my legs to the side, to the left of the brake pedal so they wouldn't touch the brakes. In the van I drive today, the hand controls are not connected to the gas and the brake, so I don't have to worry about that: my van is still a regular van, but I have a brake pad so I don't have to worry about my feet getting in the way when I'm using the hand controls. And Joe is the only one who can drive my van with the hand controls.

When I got behind the wheel and started driving, I couldn't believe I was actually driving *a real car*. Do you know how freeing that was? It was so amazing. Lynne was really cautious with me, especially during our first lessons. She made sure I stopped at every yellow light, for example, and she never turned on the radio. She did not want me to have any distractions.

Lynne was very patient with me and very encouraging; in fact, I was harder on myself than she was on me. I got upset with myself for not being able to drive better. One time, as I was pulling into my driveway, I saw Joe's mom and dad were outside, with his sister. I got nervous because I knew they would be watching me pull in, so of course, since I was nervous, I jerked a little bit, and I did not pull in as smoothly as I wanted to. Nothing happened to the car; I did not hit anything or run over anything; the car was just a little crooked. But I started crying and banging on the steering wheel because I was so frustrated. I remember saying to Lynne, "I just want to do this right, I want to do this right, *why can't I do this right?*"

Lynne pointed out that I hadn't done anything wrong, and she reminded me that I was still learning. She also reminded me that I had already accomplished an enormous amount, just by getting *in* the car and *wanting* to learn to drive. Lynne was great that way: she helped me see my accomplishments, and she refused to listen to me complain about my failures or difficulties. We all have difficulties—even people who don't have the physical limitations I do—and I need to keep that in mind, in everything I do.

I took lessons with her for about six months. I had lessons three or four days a week, and each lesson was about three hours, so there was a lot of driving time. Then, of course, I had to take my driver's test. That was a funny day. The driving test was so easy, but it was also hard, because I was so nervous. But it was a breeze: I had no trouble doing the K turn or getting into a parking spot. I passed, and I was thrilled!

I took my driver's test at the same place everyone does; there's just a separate part for driving a car with hand controls. The funny part was that, after I passed the driving test, I had to go into the building to get my driver's license—and that's when I realized I had forgotten to bring my wheelchair! I don't know what I was thinking when I left the house that morning: I guess I was so excited when Lynne picked me up to take me for the test, that it just completely slipped my mind to bring my wheelchair. After all, I thought I'd be in the car the whole time. I did not even have my walker, so I did not know how I was going to get to the office to pick up my license. But nothing was going to stop me from getting it that day, that was for sure!

So Lynne had a bright idea. She went into the building and brought a rolling chair—from one of the offices—outside in the parking lot for me, and she rolled me through the hallways until we got to the department where I could get my license. She kept saying to me, "Hold on, Theresa, hold on!" People were looking at us as though we were goofing around, but we thought it was so funny. We were laughing our heads off, and. I was smiling from ear to ear. I was so happy that day, because I knew I had achieved another milestone towards living a more independent life!

That night, Joe, Samantha, and I celebrated. Joe made a beautiful dinner for me, and I called everybody to tell them the good news. I was on the phone almost the whole night. Everyone was so happy for me when I passed the driving test, and I was happiest of all, because I knew this was going to be a new chapter in my life.

A few weeks later, Joe and I bought the van I drive today. It's specially made, with hand controls only, which are connected to the gas and brake. It also has a brake and gas pad to prevent me from pushing on the gas and brake pedals with my feet. There's also a ramp inside, so I can get in while still on my scooter. I just push a button on my car keys, the ramp comes down, the scooter goes up the ramp, inside the van, and then I maneuver out of the scooter, into the driver's seat. My scooter goes between the back seat and the front seat in the van. Then the ramp goes up.

The van was specially made for me. You have to know how to drive with hand controls in order to drive it. Joe knows how to drive with my hand controls, so he drives it occasionally, but I don't let anyone else drive my van, because they don't know how to drive it.

* * * * *

My confidence about my driving ability was tested one day, and I believe that test proved that I was right about myself. I was driving home from Delaware on a cloudy, chilly day, and while I was driving, this placid and easygoing feeling came over me. Then I felt chills running all throughout my body. Then this little whisper from within me told me to make sure I slowed down when getting off the Commodore Barry Bridge, which connects Pennsylvania and New Jersey, just south of Philadelphia.

So I listened to my voice within and made sure I slowed down when I got off the bridge. I slowed down quite a bit. I was on a three-lane highway, and I was in the middle lane, with two cars next to me, one on each side. Then the car next to mine, in the left lane, skidded on a patch of ice. But I did not panic at all. It seemed like my vehicle and I became frozen in time: I saw everything in slow motion right before my eyes. It was as though my vehicle simply stopped, but I did not put on my brakes. I just remember seeing the car that had been in the left lane skidding and swerving right in front of my vehicle in the middle lane, missing my van by mere inches. Then it swerved into the right lane, hitting the car that was on the other side of my vehicle. But my car was untouched!

The two cars that collided pulled over onto the side of the road, and I stopped as well because I felt I was involved somehow, and I did not want to leave the scene of a car accident. My nerves and stomach were quivering with shock and fear of what might have happened to me. I couldn't believe my van hadn't gotten hit and that I had prevented that from happening to me. When the police showed up, they were shocked as well!

Still, I was very nervous about continuing to drive home. So I called my mother-in-law to pick me up and take me home. When she got there, she was so surprised that I had prevented my van from getting hit. She talked to the police, who told her how I did such a great job by not being startled and preventing a more serious accident. The police told her they were so proud of me and that I had handled the situation very well!!

My mother-in-law asked me if I wanted to drive myself home or if I wanted her to take me home. I kept going back and forth with the idea of her taking me home because I was so worried this was going to happen again, but I realized this almost-accident couldn't hold me back from driving. I couldn't be scared or nervous: I came too far to where I want to be in my life. So I told my mother-in-law that I would drive myself home, and she asked, "Are you sure?" I said, "Yes, I was sure," so she said, "OK." She had this worried look on her face, but she also gave me confidence that I could drive home because she told me how proud she was of me for not getting hit and not getting startled when the car in front of me skidded and swerved and hit the car on the other side of me.

I started to drive myself home on that cold wintry day when all of sudden, I looked on the bottom of my windshield and I saw a white praying mantis. I thought out loud, *this can't be – No way! Am I seeing right, because it's so cold outside, how could there be a white praying mantis on my windshield?* Plus, I had never seen a white praying mantis in my life! Then right away, I thought, *you're here, aren't you? Oh My Gosh! You're letting me know you're here. It's a sign from God! You're a sign from God – Thank you! Thank you, God!* I blew a kiss, and then the praying mantis flew away. I know this was truly an amazing blessing from God and Daddy and my angels above!!!

*   *   *   *   *

Other than that one time, I'm happy to say that I haven't had any problems driving. I'm very fortunate—and I'm a good driver. I'm very careful. Interestingly, I have more problems in parking lots than I do on the road! I've encountered a lot of people who are not really respectful of the handicapped parking places.

One time, I was in a parking lot, and I parked in a handicapped spot, but there wasn't enough room for me to get out of my van, because I need room for the ramp to come down from the van. So I couldn't park there after all. When that happens, I have to park in a regular spot, but then I worry about how I'll get back into my van if someone parks next to me, because the ramp is six feet long, so I need a lot of clearance next to me to accommodate that. In fact, there's even a sign on my van that reads "please park at least 8 feet away from this van"—but people either don't notice it or don't care.

Another time, I was parked in a handicapped parking place, and when I came back out to my van, I saw that someone had parked right next to my van, on the painted blue lines—which are there for a reason—so no-one will park there! If you've never been handicapped or disabled, you probably never thought about those blue lines before or why they were there, and the reason is, to accommodate ramps like mine and to have room for wheelchairs, too. I wanted to call the police, because it's illegal to park there, but I did not. Instead, I just went back inside the store and told the security guards. One of the guards had to back my van out of the tight space, which was hard for him to do because he did not know how to use the hand controls. And this has happened to me so many times.

Another time, I was at the hospital, with my brother-in-law Luis and his 23-year-old daughter Melina; we were visiting my mother, who was very sick. I thought she was dying, and I was terribly worried about her. I stayed with her every day as long as I could, so I did not come back outside until about 9:00 at night, and the same thing had happened to me: someone had parked in the blue lines, next to me. Thank God Luis and Melina saw that, because I was ready to push the button on my car keys to activate the ramp to come down, and the ramp would have hit the car next to me, and it would have done a lot of damage. I was so upset and so shocked that someone had the audacity to do that—especially at a *hospital*, of all places, where there are understandably many people who *need* to park in the handicapped spaces.

All I wanted to do that night was go home to be with Samantha and Joe: I was so upset about my mother's condition, and I just wanted to get home. And Luis and Melina were so mad that someone had blocked me in. My niece Melina said I should call the police, but again, I did not want to do that. So she left a note on the car's windshield, letting them know the situation they put me in and that they shouldn't park where they're not supposed to, especially in the handicapped section! I was lucky that Luis was able to back my car out of the space so I could go home.

Because of all these parking difficulties, I often can't find a place to park, so I double-park. One time, I went to the grocery store, and there were no parking spots, so I was double-parked. I had no choice. Then a man pulled up beside me and said, "What are you doing? What gives *you* the right to park here?" So I rolled down my window and said, "I'm handicapped!" And he started cursing me out! I was actually frightened that he was going to try to hurt me in some way: he got out of his car and started to come toward me, still cursing at me. I quickly rolled up my window, and I kept saying "I'm handicapped" but he did not care. Finally, he left me alone and got back in his car and drove off. Still, I was pretty shaken up: I don't see why people can't be more understanding of my situation, or have a little compassion. It's not like I'm *not* handicapped and just trying to park in a handicapped space.

Another time I was at a shopping center and there were no handicapped spots left, so I again double-parked. And when I came out, there was a note on my windshield that said, "Why do you think your van is so special that you can double-park?" I just crumpled it up and threw it away, but it makes me sad that there are people who can be so unkind. Some people just don't care that I'm handicapped.

A few months ago, I was driving through a parking lot at Kohl's, and there was one handicapped spot left. I saw there was another car—a truck, actually—behind me, but somehow the other car got to that space before me. So I blew my horn at her. I parked my van in another space, and when I got out of the van, she was waiting in her truck for me. When she got out of her truck, she walked perfectly fine, she was young, and there did not seem to be anything wrong with her. There also wasn't a handicapped placard in her truck—at least, I did not see one. Then she asked me, "What the bonkers are you doing, blowing your horn at me?" I said, "you know I wanted that spot, and you can walk. I have a special van with a ramp and a scooter because I can't walk." At that, she said, "So what? Just because you're handicapped, you think the world owes you? So what?" I started crying. Then she literally *ran* inside the store.

So I went to the manager, because he knows me, and I told him what happened. He felt so bad for me. All the stuff I go through, my life, what I have to deal with, what I have to put up with. I kept saying, "I don't understand." I just did not get why she needed to be so mean to me.

There are some cruel people in the world: they think only about themselves, and they don't care about anyone else. They don't care what other people go through. I lost my cool with her...because she really crushed my heart. I need to be stronger, to not let people like her affect me. That's another reason I'm writing this book: to help people realize that they need to be strong, and realize that every one of us has power within us to achieve our goals and be the person we want to be. I'm working on that: I drive every day— and I'm glad I'm able to do that now. I'm glad I'm more independent, and I just try to live every day without the rest of the world bringing me down.

* * * * *

A few months later, I had another important experience while I was driving—this time much happier than the accident on the highway. I was leaving A.I. DuPont from helping out with Healing Touch and I was heading to my van in the parking lot, when I noticed a woman was following me. Then she approached me and asked me, "How did you get here?" I said, "I drive. "She said, "you *drive?*" She had such a dumbfounded, surprised look on her face when I told her I drive. She couldn't figure out how I could drive because I am disabled. She asked me, "How can you drive?" I told her I drive with my hands, using hand controls. She said, "I have an eighteen-year-old daughter who is paralyzed from the waist down, and she is so closed up: she always wants to stay in the house and do nothing. She is so depressed, and I am trying to figure out a way for her to do things and be as independent as possible and to open up her world with possibilities to have her dreams come true."

I took her to my van and I showed her my hand controls, how I maneuver my seat, and how my ramp works so I can get into the van. Then we both sat in the van and talked. She asked me how I overcame my situation and accepted it to get where I am today. I told her, "I've gotten to where I am today because of the power in believing and having faith and because of the love of my whole entire family. They gave me the strength, power, and encouragement that nothing is impossible. My two most important examples were my mother and father. That's what you have to give your daughter: tremendous encouragement that *nothing is impossible.* Show her the power of believing in herself to never give up and to be proud of who she is. That her dreams and goals can come true one way or the other. That "impossible" can become *possible!* I can't emphasize enough how you and her father are her prime examples in life, and if you both show her and make her aware of all your love and support and strengths of faith, then those qualities will be embedded inside her and help her to live a happy, fulfilling and successful life. *You need to be strong for your daughter.* Be her best example of what her life could be. Make her aware of what power she has inside her. Ignite that flame within her! I have a daughter, and I'm the one with the disability, but I have to be strong for her because I want to be the best example for *her*. I want her to see that if her Mommy can do things and overcome an obstacle or hurdle that's in my way, then so can *she*!!! BE STRONG!!!"

She took a deep breath and then exhaled while tears fell from her eyes. She said, "Thank you so much, you made me have so much clarity and insight of what potential and possibilities my daughter has in her life. She has the power to make her life become however she wants it to be, and her father and I will be guiding her with love and support and strengthening her with encouragement every step of the way. We'll be right beside her." Then she gave me the biggest hug!!!

Ever since I talked to that beautiful mother, she opened up my eyes of what God's plans are for me to do. I felt the most powerful, rewarding feeling that day, after I helped that woman become aware of the power and potential her daughter has—and the power *she* has, as her mother, of being the prime example for her daughter. It felt so right to help her, and I just knew without a doubt in my heart that this was God's intention.

JOINING A GYM—AND BEING TOLD "YOU DON'T BELONG HERE"

AFTER I STARTED DRIVING, I returned to physical therapy for a few months, but after several sessions, the therapists felt I wasn't getting any better, so they told me there was no need to come back. I had begun to feel some improvement in myself, too, but when my therapists told this to my insurance company, the insurance company dropped me and stopped paying for therapy! I was so upset and really angry. I thought to myself, *this is not going to stop me; I am not going to give up! NO WAY!! If I do that, then my body is going to get worse and deteriorate. I've got my daughter to think about, and I want to do things and take care of her the best that I can.*

So I decided to try going to the gym where my husband used to take me before I started driving. Unfortunately, my first and only day at this gym was degrading: I was working out on the leg press machine when the manager came over to me and told me I needed to get off. He said, "You don't belong here." I said, "What?" He said, "You don't belong here. If anything happens to you, we are responsible." I told him, "I'm responsible for myself." He said, "No you're not, *we* are. How did you even get here?" I said, "I drove here myself." Apparently, when I came to the gym with Joe, the gym did not mind, but since I had come alone this time, they were worried that something would happen to me, and they would be liable.

He then told me again to get off the machine. I refused and accused him of discrimination. "Call my husband," I told him, which he did. Joe was caught in the middle of the situation. The manager at the gym thought he was absolutely right and that I did not belong in the gym unless somebody was with me. I felt like this was a horrible nightmare. I actually couldn't believe this was real and that it was happening to me. I was actually getting kicked out of a place because of my disability!

I got off the machine. But then I thought to myself, *This isn't right. God, help me! Please help me. Is this how it's going to be for the rest of my life? Dealing with situations and people who make me feel like less of a person just because I have a disability? Why, God, why me? Am I always going to be judged or labeled?* Then myself-pity turned into self-*strength*. I thought that I had to be emotionally strong and not put up with it. I had worked very hard to get where I was, and I wasn't going to have anybody destroy that!

So I got the disability rights activists involved—and a year later, the gym was no longer in business, for reasons unknown. Today, I go to another gym because I am not going to give up on myself, physically or mentally, in terms of my self-esteem. It's been hard at times, but I know I have the inner strength to keep going! That is what my life and future are all about. To move forward each and every single day and to do my best and never give up even when life gets tough.

The gym I go to now is LA Fitness. I go primarily to use the leg-press machine. I do about 120 or 130 leg presses in 30 to 45 minutes. While I'm doing them, my heart beats so fast, and I lose myself. I think of when I was a kid, before my aneurysm, when I used to run through fields on our farm, when I felt so free. Now, I can't even use the treadmill, because I can't walk. Working out brings back those memories of when I was able-bodied and not limited.

Every once in a while, I get depressed when I see all the other people at the gym who are able-bodied and not limited at all, who can work out on whatever machine they want to or do any type of exercise they enjoy. I find myself wishing I was able-bodied, the way I used to be. One time when I was doing leg presses, another girl was using the rowing machine, and I watched her as she bent her legs all the way to her chest. I can't do that, so watching her just really got to me, and I put my head down between my knees and cried. After a few minutes, I forced myself to stop crying, and I picked my head up and went back to working out. I did not want anyone to see me crying.

I need to be strong, I need to focus, and I can't let other people bother me. I'm not going to let my feelings stop me from what I want to do. I'm proud of myself for going to the gym. But it does get to me at times, seeing all the able-bodied people; sometimes, I dread going to the gym. I have my ups and downs, and when I'm down, I have to pick myself back up. Friends have suggested I go with someone, thinking it would be more fun for me to have a gym buddy. But I prefer to go alone because I want to get in, work out, and leave. I have my regimen: I do some arm work, and I do the leg press. Every now and then, I work with a trainer.

I like going to LA Fitness because the trainers are so incredible. I can't get on the leg machine by myself, and they always help me. The people at LA Fitness help me get on the machines: they grab one leg, swing it over, and put it onto the machine, then they hold on to my arms and pull me up. Then I sit down. The trainers just come over to help me, I don't even have to ask them anymore. They know the weight I use—either 75 or 90 pounds. I work out for 30-45 minutes, and a lot of the people who go to my gym know that when I'm there, they need to stay away from the leg press—because it's *my* leg press. Everyone is really nice to me there.

One trainer in particular, named Aaron, was so wonderful to me: he made me stand by myself and walk by myself. I did not want to because I was self-conscious: everybody was watching me. But he walked behind me saying, "Theresa, you can do this. I'll be right behind you, in case you fall." So I took a couple of steps, and then

I walked a few more steps. He did not have to help me, but he did, and his encouragement was the greatest gift he could have given me.

I'm determined to get better, one way or another, and I don't want to lose the strength I have; I don't want to deteriorate and get any worse!

DISCOVERING THE "HEALING TOUCH"

WHILE I WAS WORKING AT the hospital, one of my co-workers, Lisa, asked me if I wanted to see Walle(pronounced *Wally*) and do "Healing Touch" on my lunch break. Lisa said, "She might help you because you seem uptight." I knew she did not mean this in a bad way, and even though I did not know what "Healing Touch" was, I said I would go, so Lisa made an appointment for me at noon. Walle came and got me because I wasn't too sure where her office was.

When we got to Walle's office, we talked for a bit and she asked me if I have any pain or troubles from within. I told her a few of my troubles and worries about my physical condition and she said, "I'll help you: Healing Touch will help you!" She helped me onto the Healing Touch table—which is just like a massage table—and she told me to close my eyes and take a deep breath and have faith. She said, "You are here to put your mind in a relaxed comfort zone, to let go of all your worries and stress. I'll do all the rest and the work for you to let it go."

The room was dim, with soothing music, and she started to do her work. It's energy medicine or field therapy. It help centers your core and gets you grounded. It's a technique in which the hands are directed to use human energy for healing purposes. There is no actual physical contact.

While she was doing her work, I felt like my heart and soul and mind were unfolding, with beautiful flowers before me. My Dad actually came to me, and I saw him right beside me, and he told me to *be strong, be brave for Samantha, find your core, the power within you, and never, ever give up, Theresa. I'll always be right here with you – You're not alone!!! God has his hands on you, and he has great and wonderful things for you to do.* Then I saw myself walking on the beach, without my walker, holding onto my precious Samantha's hand with my Dad also beside me. It felt so real.

I did not want those moments to go away. In my mind, my heart and soul they were as authentic as a beautiful genuine diamond. Then my mind, heart, and soul were brought back in the room, Daddy was standing over me, tears rolling down my face. Daddy leaned over and grabbed my hand and with a whisper from within, he said, *I love you, Theresa!!!* I said, "I love you, too, Daddy." Then he said, *I have to go.* I said, "Don't go, Daddy don't go! Don't go!" But his hand drifted off my hand, and then he faded away...with the angels and spirits!!!

Walle is a beautiful woman inside and out. She and Healing Touch made me aware of so many things about what my life is really all about, what God's plan is for me and His intentions (my missions), and answers for why I became disabled. It awakened those parts that were broken inside and put the pieces of my unfinished puzzle back together. Healing Touch gave me a whole different outlook on coming together with my spirits and angels; it also shed light on my Daddy's continued presence in my life. My angels will always remind me of the qualities I have inside me, so I can keep going and achieve my life's purpose. One day, I envision myself in the heavenly heavens: I'll be surrounded by the Lord's glory and I'll be dancing with my Dad and with the angels!!!

I healed with the help of Healing Touch, which is energy work—a holistic approach to health that honors the complete person from a mind-body-spirit perspective. It gave me such clarity regarding what I needed to do to succeed after I suffered this life-changing event. It rekindled and recaptured my inner spirit and strengths. Healing Touch made me realize what I needed to do to put the pieces of my life back together, how to open my heart, and be a complete person, not just a person with a disability.

GOING BACK TO WORK

I HAD STOPPED WORKING WHEN Samantha was born, but when she was almost finished preschool, I decided to go back to work at the A. I. DuPont Children's Hospital. I was hoping to find a job that involved helping children, especially children suffering from problems like mine, since I certainly know quite a bit about overcoming disability! So I again talked to the president about helping me, and he found me a job in one of the departments in the hospital that was close to the patient ward.

When the president got me this job, I was so overwhelmed with excitement about working at the Hospital again and hoping to help children and others. He made my Dream Come True! That meant so much to me because he did not have any Doubts in my ability.

I worked there for about two and a half years, until I was laid off. I hung in there until the very end. I tried my hardest to go above and beyond whatever they asked me to do: I truly wanted to help out in that department in any way I could, and I wanted to further my skills in that job. I felt I had so much to give and offer to the hospital for the patients, and the parents, and my co-workers. But it seemed to me that my co-workers and one of my new supervisors did not give me the chance to help out more and to get more working hours. I tried to prove myself, but I felt a great deal of animosity towards me from the people in the department. Even while I was enduring such negative circumstances, though, I still tried to maintain a positive energy. I couldn't just give up—on myself, or the job at the hospital. I am proud of the work I did there, in spite of everything was happening.

One day, I tried talking to the new supervisor, but the first thing she said to me was, "The president of the hospital helped you get this job"—which was true, and I did not see anything wrong with that! Then she said, "Ah, you're pretty..."I did not expect that from her, and I thought it was so unprofessional for her to say that. I was so stunned; I did not reply anything back to her.

I also tried to think positive, and I tried so hard to get along with my co-workers. I understand that I may have not gone through all the procedures to get my job. But I felt that my coworkers were frustrated with me because they had to go through more to get their positions.

I tried to get another position in the hospital so I could get away from all that negativity in the office. I again went to the president of the hospital and talked to him about my position and about looking for another job in the hospital. I asked him if he could help me find a position in the hospital where I could talk to children about dealing with their disabilities. I wanted to help children who were patients at the hospital understand that they could have happy, successful, and fulfilling lives, and I wanted to help put their parents' minds at ease about what their children's capabilities were. He tried to help me with this idea, but he had only a short amount of time before he retired. He did find a position where I could help with the children, but it did not work out because of certain rules and regulations of the hospital.

After, he retired I went to see one of the higher up executives and asked him if there was any way he could create a *new* department in the hospital where I could help out with the children and their parents, with whatever situation they were dealing with in their lives. He told me it was a great idea, but I needed to write a proposal explaining my plan. He told me he would see what he could do, and he would get back to me right away. In fact, he told me one of his secretaries would call me in a week to let me know what was happening with my idea. *WOW!!!* I was so excited and overwhelmed, and I had such high hopes that my life's mission and God's plan was going to come true in my life. I was creating visions in my mind that one day in this hospital, I would have such an incredible, rewarding gift of being able to help other children and their parents and anyone else affected by disability. My heart was literally pitter pattering with excitement!

I waited for one of his secretaries to call me that Monday, but no-one ever did.

I did not get a return phone call. So I called him a few days later. When a secretary picked up, I asked her about what the higher executive had told me, about creating a new department in the hospital to give children and their parents help through certain crises and with children's disabilities. I was absolutely floored by what she said to me: "The higher executive said that you and your kind of people need to be more educated before you think you can help other people with certain disabilities and crises."

When I heard that, my heart felt like it crumbled into thousands of pieces. I couldn't believe those words came out of her mouth. I even asked her to repeat what she said because I thought I had heard wrong. But I had heard right, and she thought there was nothing wrong with what she had said to me. I struggled within and tried to talk to her. The first thought that came to my mind was *this is a hospital—a children's hospital—dealing with children who have all kinds of disabilities.* What she said to me kept rumbling through my head: "Your kind of people needs to be more educated." I couldn't concentrate on anything else, so I left right away to go to the hospital to see her in person because I wanted some clarification.

On the way there, I got stopped by a police officer. I was going 70 in a 55-mile speed limit. I told the officer my situation and that I hadn't realized I was going that fast, and I promised it wouldn't happen again. He said, "You're lucky I know who you are, because I see you at the gym a lot. I'll give you a warning this time, but next time I catch you speeding, you might not be as lucky!"

I said, "Thank you, thank you, Officer."

After that happened and the police officer drove off, I sat there in my van and contemplated for a few minutes. I thought to myself, *is this a sign from God to stop me from going to the hospital?* My heart was so torn and confused that I dismissed that thought from my mind and I continued on my way to the hospital.

When I arrived at the hospital, I went straight to the higher executive's office. One of the secretaries stopped me and asked me, "Why are you here, Theresa?"

I was boiling with so much steam of disappointment in my heart, so I told her, "I want to see and speak to the higher executive, and if he won't see me, I am going to call Channel Six News!"

She said, "What?"

I said. "You heard me: I'll call Channel Six News!" She asked, "Is that a threat?" When she said that, I calmed down because I did not want it to be a threat, but I was so confused and distressed. I just couldn't understand how anyone in their right mind—especially someone in such a position at a hospital, would ever say to somebody, "Your kind of people need to be more educated!"

The reason for my distress was that I just wanted someone to understand my thoughts and feelings. I had no intention of threatening anyone, but I see how it could have come across as a threat. I just loved the hospital so much, and my heart was being torn: it actually felt like I was being ripped away from my sanctuary. I felt so strongly, from deep within me, that I needed to be there, and I was trying to express how much I appreciate and recognize the value of being an employee there. I was also trying to make the higher executive aware of how I felt. I did not want him to take this secure feeling away from me. I wanted him to know I could work just as well as anybody else, with or without a disability.

So I asked if I could speak to another higher person about this matter, and the secretary told me she was having lunch. At this, she walked into the office, and I got the chance to talk to her and explain the reason I acted the way I did and what the secretary had said to me. I was bawling my eyes out to her explaining my side of the story, and I told her I was not going to call Channel Six News because she was really worried about that and the hospital's reputation.

I tried to explain to her that I did not understand why I was having so much difficulty fitting in my department at the hospital. I told her I always went above and beyond for this hospital and how ever since I came back to work in this new position, it had been *torture for me.* I told her that I had been working overall here for 10 years; I said, "This place is like my second home, and all I want to do is be able to help others with their trials in their life, and show them how they can overcome their disabilities and succeed. That is why I am going to college now and volunteering and reaching out to others." Then I asked her, "Why is everyone here making it *so hard* for me? This is what I want to do, and I know this is what God's plans are for me! This is my life's *mission*!!!I don't *want* to leave this hospital. I know *this* is where I am supposed to be."

When I had finished talking, she said, "Theresa, maybe you should look elsewhere to help others. This isn't the only place." When she said that, I looked out her office window and started to cry again while I said, "But this is where I belong: I have so many happy memories here, and I want to create new happy memories for myself and for my daughter to be proud that this is where her Mommy works. Hopefully, she'll want to volunteer here one day and want to help others. I want my daughter to have a broader view of life and understand that each and every person may be different, but we are also all the same in this world!!!"

She did not say much after that, but she was very nice and very concerned about what I had to say. She told me she would have a meeting to see what she could do for me to get my foot in the door of a new position in the hospital.

Then as I was leaving her office, the secretary who I had first confronted was waiting for me, to open the door to let me out. She took that opportunity to continue her tirade against me: she said, "Theresa, you have to understand that I got where I am today because I worked hard and because I have experience." She was going off on me like I was brainless and as though I had no experience. There was a part of me that wanted to reply to her, however, I heard a whisper from within telling me, *it's OK, Theresa. You need to overlook what she said. You need to hold on even stronger within your heart's power, believe and have faith, embrace and trust in God because this is your mission. God has plans for you and don't give up. The pieces will unfold and show where you should be. It might not be this hospital...But somehow, someway, you will succeed wherever or however you want to be because you are not a quitter!* I thought all of this, but all I said to her was "Thank you."

I do work very hard, and I have a great deal of experience, to a certain degree. I would have even more experience and knowledge in the office if they gave more work and greater responsibilities, and more working hours. My new supervisor knew I wanted more hours in the office, but she wasn't willing to give me that chance!

My main goal is I want to help people who have limitations— and able-bodied people, too—to make them aware of the possibilities they have in their life. I want to show them that they can achieve their dreams and goals by finding the power within themselves.

*   *   *   *   *

After this happened, I continued working in the office a few hours a week, but the situation was getting worse and worse. Also, the atmosphere with my co-workers was getting uncomfortable for me because they had to find work that I was able to do and they were hiring other people. Still, I was trying so hard to hang in there and keep my casual part-time job in the hospital. I just felt in my heart that I couldn't be a quitter. I wasn't going to quit my job and give up on myself because I was hoping my supervisor would see how much effort I was putting into my work.

Then one morning, I came into the office to work, and the new supervisor came up to me. She said, in front of everyone who was in that office that morning, "Theresa, the higher person that you spoke to and a few others had a meeting about you, and we all agreed that we would help you find another position in the hospital where you could get more hours." "We're also on the lookout for any positions in the hospital where you could help out with the children and make them realize what possibilities they have."

When the new supervisor said that, I was beside myself and smiling from cheek to cheek. But when she saw the expression on my face and how happy I was, she added, "No promises, Theresa." I feared for the worst!

A couple of days later, that same supervisor set up a meeting with me and her and one of the recruiters. At that meeting, I explained to them that I have a great deal of experience in data entry, because I had worked in Hospital Medical Billing for eight years, and before that, I had volunteered in the Medical Records department for almost 2 years. I told them that I would love to get more experience in the department I was already working in, but it was so hard because I was been given so few hours to work. In other words, if I couldn't work more, I would never be able to succeed, and get where I want to be. What's more, I told them I was going to college and doing volunteer work in the Special Needs Department at the campus.

When I finished talking, I felt they were gearing up to tell me that I should just find a job at the college campus. My heart was aching so much! I told them, "I've been working here for over ten years in this hospital, and I feel *this* is where my heart belongs, and I know I would be such a big help if there were any way possible for me to get a job helping the children in this hospital. If that's not possible, I'd be happy to work in any kind of job here for now, if I had more hours. That way, I could work up to where I want to be in this hospital."

They really did not reply anything to that. So the meeting just ended.

A few days later, right before Christmas, I was getting ready to leave the office for the day. That same supervisor came out of her office and told me, "Theresa, before you come in again, call the office first to see if there is any work for you to do." I instantly panicked and felt so anxious. So, I rushed to see the recruiter I had met with a few days earlier. I told her what happened, crying my eyes out and saying I did not understand. She said, "Theresa, whatever job you want, YOU NEED A COLLEGE DEGREE."

I said, "Even for a data entry job?"

She said, "YES!"

"But I worked in Accounts Payable (in the hospital's billing department) in data entry 3 or 4 days a week for 8 years: doesn't that count?"

She said, "No, you still need a college degree."

I said, "But, I am going to college, doesn't that matter?" She said, "No!"

Then I asked her, "Do I still have a job in the department?" At that, she told me, "I am afraid not, Theresa."

What really boggled my mind about this conversation was that I was crying my heart out, pouring my soul out to her, and she did not even say a kind word or even look at me while she was talking. With that, she turned back to her computer and started to work. I was left with a sense of despair. She made me feel so small and her presence and actions towards me felt as though I was nothing. She did ask me if I was OK to drive home. Still, her behavior was so merciless towards me because she was so callous and uncaring.

* * * * *

Ironically, before they laid me off, I had gotten a letter in the mail from the hospital, inviting me to my Tenth Year Award Ceremony. I was so excited to attend, because I was so proud that I had been working there for ten years. But after I got laid off, I couldn't believe this was happening to me. I asked God, *how much more pain and* agony can I take? Why, God? I don't get it! My heart is always breaking, and I try *so incredibly hard* to overcome and accomplish what I want to be in my life, and I try to put aside whatever negativity that gets in my way. Is this what my life is all about? To see how strong I am, God? Is this a test? I was so angry.

Then my anger subsided, and I thought the test is the power of believing and having faith and being proud. I thought *as long as I shall live, I will never give up, and I will beat this storm that's in my way and be proud. I will testify to God's love, and I will defeat this one way or another. He's holding my hand, guiding me every step of the way to enlighten my heart in so many ways, to enrich my world!*

So I went to my Tenth Year Award Ceremony, even though I had been laid off. It took a lot to conceal my feelings, because my heart was full of tremendous sadness, especially when I saw that everyone else was so happy. But just knowing I was there(with tears, but still there!) and knowing that I had stood my ground, that enabled me to be so proud of this hospital and that I had gotten this far in my life. I did not let my obstacles or anyone stop me from what I want to accomplish, and that my knowledge and wisdom gives me the strength to find courage within myself!

My heart keeps telling me, *don't give up! Don't let obstacles and hurdles discourage you. Keep pursuing your life's mission. Follow your heart!* So after the awards ceremony, I talked to the higher administrators of the hospital, about possibly starting new guidance programs for children who were patients and for their parents. I wanted to call them "The Child Transition Support Program" and "The Parents' Transition Support Program," and I wrote a proposal describing how they would work.

I believed the children's support program would help children by encouraging them to believe in themselves, to have confidence, to persevere, and to find their inner strength. I wanted to show children that they can overcome the obstacles and hurdles that will face them in the future. I wanted to help other patients learn to live happy, fulfilling, and successful lives. I wanted to help them understand that people with disabilities are no different from anybody else: we all are unique and different in our own way, and each and every one of us has some kind of disability, mentally or physically, because nobody is perfect. I wanted these programs to help children find their inner core within themselves and to focus on the positive, rather than the negative, and especially to help them be proud of who they are.

I also believed that the parents' support program would help put their minds at ease about their children. I wanted the program to help parents realize that they are the prime examples for their children's lives, to make parents aware that their children's lives can be happy, fulfilling, and successful—that their dreams can come true, one way or another. Both programs would help diminish the negative circumstances in their lives and help them focus on the positive conditions. I believed the programs could have a vast impact on changing the attitudes of the patients and their families by encouraging their self-esteem, their self-worth, and their overall well-being. I wanted to help them see the light and understand that they have the power within them to be happy.

My feelings about this were—and still are—so potent that I just can't let go of this idea. I know all the obstacles and the hurdles I overcame and the things I achieved were for a reason. There is no doubt in my mind that all of my life experiences were lessons—lessons that I am supposed to help and share with others.

Unfortunately, I was unable in my objective to convince the hospital to establish these programs, but I haven't given up on the idea yet. I continue to hope that someone will recognize that they would be a valuable addition to the hospital's resource center. And until that happens, I'll continue to work on achieving other goals in my life.

GOING TO COLLEGE AND PURSUING NEW GOALS

TODAY AS I LOOK BACK, I know I've been through a lot of situations and barriers that I have had to overcome and deal with. It's been a hard road for me, but since I have been doing Healing Touch with Walle's help, there is no longer doubt in my mind that all of these life experiences are my lessons – lessons that will help me to be a much stronger person and to be proud of who I am. Healing Touch gave me such overwhelming tranquility and empowered me with strength and confidence. It allowed me to clear my mind, to think about the absolute positive energy in life, and to turn away from the negative energy that was cast in my head.

I have decided that whatever is negative in your life, you can turn it into a positive if you stay focused on that. My ambitions, motivation, and perseverance were always present in my heart. I would feel them close, but I would get discouraged and let them go. They were within me from the time I was a little girl and as I grew up with my family, and the two most important living examples of that faith were my mother and father. Healing Touch reconnected me with my source and re-ignited that place in my heart. Now I want to grasp and embrace it and hold it close forever.

This was God's plan, and He has guided me down the path where I need to go. God is giving me the courage, as my inner spirit helps me to move forward to do the things I need to do and the things I came to do. When I am on the Healing Touch table, I go to another place in my heart and to another world. It is hard to describe it, but I get in touch with my inner spirits. I just want to keep those miraculous visions as my links to my faith. Nothing is impossible. All you need to do is believe and open your heart to the wonders of what this remarkable life is all about and what life has ready for you to follow your dream of dreams.

Today, I am attending college. My dream and goal is to earn a degree in psychology and counseling. I would like to encourage others who feel that their disabilities limit them from finding happiness in life, and let them know that is so not true. Life doesn't stop just because you have a disability, and I am proof of that!

I want to do so many *more* things with my life, which is one of the reasons I started college. I decided to go to college when I was working at the hospital one day: I had an epiphany. I saw all the young medical students, and I thought, *I'm not too old to get my degree. I'm not going to give up. I can do this!* I saw the students, and I thought if *they* can do this, *I* can do this. It was an incredible feeling: I had chills all over my body. It was a sign from God: *Theresa, don't give up; you can do this!* God was showing me the direction I needed for my life, what I need to do to fulfill my dreams and accomplish my goals. And I'm *not* too old: people of all ages go back to college.

So in 2010, I started taking classes at Gloucester County College, now Rowan College. I'm studying psychology, but I also take other courses. I take two or three classes each semester, because I can't really handle more than that, with Samantha still so young. I go to school during the day, not at night. And I don't take any classes in the summer, because I want to be home with Samantha. I'm hoping to get my degree in two or three years.

I'm pursuing a bachelor's, but I might go even further. I love learning new things, and I find it so fascinating when the students talk to the professors. Learning is a gift! Before my accident, I did not care about school, but that's because I was only 14 years old. And after my accident, my main focus was on getting better. Then I met Joe and got married, and then I worked until I got pregnant. When Samantha was born, I took time off to take care of her, and then at the end of 2009, went back to work at the Children's Hospital Then I thought about going to college to better and broaden my horizons what was intended for me to do in this lifetime of mine. I'm so glad I made that decision.

I want to do something in child psychology or social work. Ideally, I'd like to use my degree to become a therapist and see patients. I have so much experience with overcoming obstacles in life: I know what it takes to get through. After my accident, I saw a psychologist at DuPont—several, in fact, at different times. Dr. Jane Crowley was especially remarkable and outstanding. She helped me a lot. I met with her for about three years after my accident, off and on until I finished high school. I'd like to help other people the way she helped me, which is why I decided to pursue a degree in psychology.

I was a little intimidated on my first day of classes because I did not know what to expect, especially in my position—after all, it had been a long time since I'd been in school! I had gone to vocational school for a few years after high school, but that's different from college. Plus, Joe was going to the same school with me back then; now, I was doing this alone. But I stayed positive, believing God was guiding me to where I needed to go on my life's path.

The first class I took in college was public speaking. I thought that course would help me get my voice stronger and become more confident talking to others and with children in large groups. I have difficulty talking since the aneurysm: my voice is whispery, and it's not always easy for other people to understand me. I was nervous when I first got to the classroom: I was on my scooter, and there were about 20 or 30 people in the class. Fortunately, no-one said anything to me when I scooted in. I did not want to say anything because I did not want to embarrass myself, because it was such a new experience for me. I was also happy to see I wasn't the oldest person in the class: there was a woman who had just turned 40, and she and I soon started working together. The public speaking class turned out to be so stupendous and awesome for me because I learned so much! Also, I had an out-of-this-world teacher for that class: she was really tough, but she knew exactly what she was doing to get her point across, which is obviously critical for anyone who wants to be a public speaker.

The only experience I've had with public speaking was at a seminar for disability awareness at A. I. DuPont. Dr. Alexander, who was my incredible rehab doctor at Dupont, asked me to be one of the speakers. He's in a wheelchair, too, because he had polio when he was a child. He asked me to talk about my disability at a seminar held at Thomas Jefferson Medical School, for about 150 medical students and parents. I was 15 the first time he asked me, then he asked me to do a seminar and a slide presentation at A.I. DuPont when I was 27, again for medical students and parents, about what I've accomplished and what I'm able to do.

The students and parents were so curious about my life: they asked me so many questions, about our house and how I get around, about Joe, about having children, even about how we have sex, which was a little (a lot!) embarrassing, but I understand why they wanted to know. I showed them pictures of me going to nightclubs, dancing in my wheelchair, and being all dressed up, to show them that a lot of people with disabilities do normal things. I'm *NO* different from lots of other people!

The seminar was also interesting to me because other people spoke about how people with disabilities were treated in the 1900s: they were often tortured and even killed because the public thought the lives of the disabled weren't worth anything, that we were nothing. I'd like to do more public speaking so I can teach and tell people what my life is like. That's what I *yearn* for. That's what my life is all about. I want to become a disability advocate. I'd like to do more of those seminars, but they aren't the focus of Dr. Alexander's work. He's primarily a rehab doctor; still, I'm going to try to find a way to do more things like that.

In the meantime, I try to tell as many people as I can about my life and how nothing holds me back. Just recently, I was at my gym, L.A. Fitness, and a guy came up to me when I got off one of the leg machines. He said to me, "I don't know how you do it: don't you feel sorry for yourself? I see how hard you struggle, and how hard you work. And I think to myself, *I don't even want to get out of bed!* I feel sorry for myself, and then I see all you're doing."

I told him, "I don't feel sorry for myself. This is God's plan for me; this is my purpose. I want to make the best of my situation. I don't want to give up on myself. I thank God for what I *have*. My life is so blessed. Every once in a while, I get frustrated, but in general, I'm *proud* of who I am. And even though I see people walk in here, running around, working out on the machines, doing whatever they want to do because they're able bodied, that still doesn't stop me from doing what I want to do. I believe, and I have faith. Feeling sorry for yourself doesn't help you in any way, so just stop it! I don't feel sorry for myself. What you do with your life is up to *you*: you have your own power to make the best of what *you've* got. The power is in your hands. Realize what you have, and wake up!" I said all this to him, and more.

Lots of people come up to me when I'm at the gym. I don't get annoyed, because I try to make them aware of what I can do. Another time, someone came up to me just as I was getting out of my wheelchair and said, "You inspire me." I thought that was so nice and it absolutely was the highlight of my day! Many people think that those of us with disabilities have given up on ourselves. But I haven't. I don't want to do that to myself. I want to do so many *more* things with my life, which is one of the reasons I'm going to college.

FACING NEW OBSTACLES, EVERY DAY

GOING BACK TO COLLEGE HAS been difficult for me in more ways than one, of course. In addition to being twice as old as everyone else on campus, I just have more trouble getting around campus than the average student does. For example, it's quite a hike between my classes and the parking lot, and one day, I was in a rush to leave because I needed to pick up Samantha by 3:30, when her school lets out. I got into my van with no problem, but then as I was trying to get out of my scooter and into the driver's seat, I lost my balance and fell, right in the middle between the driver's seat and the passenger seat. And there's not much room between the two seats, so I was wedged in pretty tightly. I panicked. I did not know what to do.

So I started calling for help. All these college kids were walking by, but nobody was coming to help me. A lot of classes had let out, and everyone was in a rush to get to their cars, plus there was loud music playing, so they couldn't hear me over the music. But I kept calling for help.

Then I remembered I have a button on my key ring for the horn, so I struggled to find my keys and reach that button. Still no-one came. I must have been yelling and honking for about five minutes, when finally, a girl and a guy came over to my van. They were about 18 or 19 years old, and they had heard me screaming; when they looked in the van, they saw me on the floor and they asked me, "Are you OK?" I said, "No, I'm stuck, and I can't get up!" So the guy pulled me out, and the girl helped, too. It took a few minutes, because they were being really gentle with me: they did not want to hurt me while moving me. I thanked them over and over: I told them how much I appreciated their help: they were like angels looking out for me. And I thanked God they showed up when they did!

Every day, there's an obstacle in my life. Last week, I went to a furniture store to look at lamps. There aren't many people who go to this store, so it's easy for me to get around; on the other hand, I found out the hard way that if there's no-one around, that can also be challenging for me. I drove there with no problems, but after I parked and pushed the button for the ramp to open out of my van, it did not open all the way. So I was stuck in my van: I couldn't get out! And there was nobody around.

I wondered what I could do to get someone's attention, so I pushed my panic button so the car alarm would go off, which it did for the next three or four minutes. But no-one came out of the store, and there was no-one in the parking lot. Finally, someone walked out of the store and saw what was going on—that I was stuck in the van, and she helped me out.

If I were able-bodied, I would have been able to just walk into the store. But I was stuck. I know I could have just retracted the ramp and driven home without going into that store that day, but I shouldn't have to do that. I chose not to give up, which is what I usually choose. At the same time, I want able-bodied people— and everybody—to realize how difficult my life is: that I need the strength and the will not to give up, every day.

I face obstacles like this every day. I never know what's going to happen to me. But I know I can't be afraid; I want to accomplish my dreams, so I gotta do what I gotta do.

*   *   *   *   *

I also know that I need to be ever more careful, no matter how careful I think I am already. I learned this lesson one very cold

February evening, when Joe took Samantha to choir practice at St. Clair's Church in Gibbstown, and I decided to surprise them and show up at her practice. Samantha was so excited to see me there because she wanted me to hear how she sang her solos and how much better her voice has gotten since she has been going to these choir practices. When I heard the beautiful, powerful organ and the drums beating in accompaniment, I sensed the aura's energy in the church. Then when I heard my daughter sing, my heart felt as if it were floating and dancing on a beautiful cloud.

After she was done her choir practice, Samantha decided to go home with her father and take a quick bath because she wanted her bath done before I got home. She knew I needed more time to get situated in my van, to position my body and legs in my driver's seat so I would be able to drive. If she finished her bath by the time I got home, she knew we would have a much more relaxing time together before her bedtime.

When I pulled into the driveway, Samantha and Joe were already home. They left about ten minutes before me, which I knew because I looked at the clock when they left the church parking lot. I saw Joe look out the garage door to see if I was home, then he went back to taking care of Samantha.

When I opened up my ramp door to come down, I did not realize that my ramp had not opened all the way. It was stuck on some hard ice and an uneven crack in the cement. It was very cold, icy, and dark, and all I wanted to do was get in the house because my body was shivering from head to toe. I knew that the longer I was outside in the freezing cold, the more pain I would have in my brick-stiff legs and all throughout my body. I struggled to move my body out of the driver's seat and onto my scooter. It seemed like it took so much time, and I was so focused on getting out of the van that when I finally got on my scooter, I realized I had totally forgotten to double-check whether or not my ramp was completely down. I just assumed my ramp was straight out and ready for my scooter to go down it. But it wasn't—and I did not realize it until

I started backing out onto the ramp and suddenly got stuck at the midpoint. Then I just kept going because I thought the ramp would straighten out by itself.

Boy, was I wrong! As I tried to go down the ramp, it did not straighten out at all. Then my scooter and I fell backwards, off the ramp and in mid-air, until we both slammed onto the concrete driveway. It seemed to happen in slow motion, because I fell first and hit my head on the concrete. The pain from hitting my head was so excruciating and unbearable! I actually thought my head had cracked open and that I was going to die. Then the scooter fell on top of me and hit me like a Mack truck landing on top of me. I remember feeling so scared out of my wits, crying and screaming and hoping my neighbors or Joe would hear me. But all the windows were closed, of course, because it was freezing outside.

I looked up at the stars in the dark sky and asked God why my life is so hard and why I have all these struggles. *What is my life all about, God? I am so tired of fighting!* I started screaming louder and louder because nobody was hearing me, not even Joe. Then I tried to push the scooter off me, thinking to myself, *stop crying, I can do this! Please God, help me find my strength!* At that point, I found my strength from within, and my shivering hands started moving the scooter off me.

Just as I was doing that, Joe opened the door inside the garage to check on me because he was wondering why it was taking me so long to get in inside. When he saw me lying in the middle of the driveway with the scooter on top of me, he ran toward me immediately—in his bare feet! He made sure I was OK and tried to discern whether I was hurt either by the fall from the van or by the scooter falling on top of me. He took the scooter off me and quickly picked me up, carried me inside, and laid me on the couch. I was still crying, and when Samantha saw me, she ran over to me with such a worried, scared look on her face. She kept asking, "What happened? Did Mommy fall? Is Mommy OK?"

At the same time, Joe was making sure I was OK and had no broken bones, and he was especially worried about whether I had cracked my head open. He said, "You need to stop crying and tell me what hurts," and then he shouted, "WHAT HURTS, THERESA?" He thought shouting would be the best way to get me to answer— and it was: I got a grip on myself and regained my self-control so that I was able to talk. I told him, "My body has pain all over, but my head hurts the most!" He checked my head to see if I was bleeding anywhere. He said he did not see any blood, then he said, "God, you have a hard head, Theresa," trying to be funny. I laughed a bit, and then I started to cry again. Next, he made sure I had no broken bones by touching and moving my limbs to see if I felt any pain. Joe said, "I don't think you've broken any bones, but you are going to be sore for a while." I said, "I'm in a lot pain by being so bruised, but thank God, I did not break anything!"

After that, he tried to make things lighter about my condition, both to cheer me up and to alleviate Samantha's concern, which we could see on her worried little face. He said silly things like, "That Mommy sure has a hard head" and "MOMMY IS ALIVE!" and "Samantha, you beat Mommy home—and you got your bath done before Mommy came home!" He was doing his best to make both of us laugh, and it worked! Then Joe told Samantha get an icepack out of the freezer, to put on my head. She ran right away to go get it, and then she asked me, "Where should I put it, Mommy?" I told her to put it on the back of my head, then I said, "You know I love you, Sweets," while tears flowed from my eyes. She said, "Mommy, I will always take care of you…just like you take care of me." Then, very carefully, she put the icepack on the back of my head, and I thanked her for helping to take care of me.

After this horrible and fearful ordeal, I believe this was a learning lesson from God to make me more aware. Since that night, I always –ALWAYS - check twice now before backing out of my ramp with my scooter. If this hadn't happened when and where it did—in my driveway, with my husband inside the house who could come to my rescue—it might have happened at some other time, when there was no-one around to help me. Something down the road with the same kind of situation could have turned out to be a lot worse. This was clearly a wake-up call to me, and I've heeded it ever since.

* * * * *

So many things happen to me each day, every time I go out. About a year ago, I was at my doctor's office, when I had to use the bathroom. It was a large bathroom, so there was enough room for me to go into it on my scooter. But as I was getting out of the scooter, it took off because I forgot to shut it off before trying to get off it. I fell onto the floor, really hard. I bruised my ribs, I hurt my thigh, and I was in so much pain. Then I couldn't get up, and since I had locked the door to the bathroom, the staff couldn't get in to help me. They had to break the doorknob to get me out.

I know it was my fault that this happened, and I told them that, but the doctor said, "You really should have someone with you." That really upset me: after all, it was an accident! I did not fall on purpose, of course. And I would think that a doctor, of all people, would be more understanding about my situation! But I realize now that they were only concerned for my well-being and safety and they were only trying to prevent me from getting hurt in the future.

Even large, public bathrooms are often a problem for me. There have been so many times when I've seen able-bodied people walk into a restroom and go straight to the handicapped stall. They have all the other stalls to choose from, but they decide to choose the one and only handicapped stall! I'm so baffled by this because able-bodied people can walk into any stall and go to the bathroom so easily: one, two, three, they're done and out of the restroom.

For me and for others who are handicapped, though, going to the bathroom takes a lot of time, and it's not at all easy. I cannot go into a regular stall because it is not big enough for my scooter to fit, and it doesn't have any rails for me to hold onto. And I can't simply get up out of my scooter and walk into a regular stall. So I feel especially handicapped and helpless when I have to wait for the handicapped stall because an able-bodied person has chosen it over the other stalls.

It just blows my mind that able-bodied people use the handicapped stalls so often. Then when that person walks out and sees me on a scooter, waiting, most of the time, the person will apologize. I always say, "It's OK! Thank you for being so sweet and apologizing!"

However, there are people who just don't care: I've encountered many people who are rude and don't even think twice about apologizing for using the handicapped stall. When that happens, I feel so letdown: it tears me up because I don't understand how people can be like that and not understand that other people need special help. Their actions are dispiriting to my soul, but I just have to accept their behavior, move forward, and overcome this obstacle when it confronts me. I'm determined that it will not get the better of me!

I've had difficulties even in my own bathroom, at home. Last week after I got home from my classes, I needed to do laundry. When the dryer was done, I needed to get the clothes out, and that's something that's really hard for me, because I always lose my balance. So I called Joe's mom for help, which I usually do, and she said she'd come right over. I needed to go to the bathroom, and I was washing my hands when I heard her come in; she called hello and said she would take the clothes out of the dryer and start folding them. I was rushing to get out of the bathroom when I knocked into my walker, it tipped over, and then I tipped over. I tried to hold on, but I just couldn't. I fell really hard, and I hit my head.

Joe's mom heard me fall, and when she got to the bathroom and tried to open the door to help me up, she couldn't open it. My body was wedged between the walker and the door, my head was cock-eyed, and my back was against the door, which is why she couldn't open it. I was so upset, I started screaming, "Why do these things

161

happen to me? I'm so tired of all these struggles!" Joe's mom tried to calm me down, and she called Joe's dad to come over. When he arrived, he tried to make me laugh with his silly voice, so I wouldn't be so upset. With a sly giggle, he said, "I'm here, Theresa, I'm here to save you and help you get up off this floor." He was trying to make the situation lighter. They told me to try to get the walker underneath me so they could open the door.

Suddenly, I thought of a movie I'd seen a few nights before, about Mary and the son of God. Jesus said to Mary, "Don't be afraid." And that's what I thought of while I was stuck in the bathroom: *Don't be afraid. Find your strength and courage.* And while I was thinking of that, somehow I got the walker underneath me. I don't know how I did it, but I pushed it underneath me, and I was able to push my body away from the door so they could open it. And they helped me up. I was in there for about 10-15 minutes.

I don't know what I would do without them: they've been such a blessing to Joe and me over the years. They're now in their 70s, though, and I'm lucky they're still really healthy. If Joe's mom hadn't been there, I would have been stuck in the bathroom for a lot longer, because I would have had to call someone to come help me. I always have two phones with me in my walker—two phones, in case one dies. Joe's dad bought me them: he worries about me all the time, and he realized the phones were necessary. So I'm never really alone. Still, I hate the fact that something like this happens to me almost every day.

One morning, I fell *twice.* I was getting ready to go to the gym to work out, and I was going to drop off Samantha at her Aunt Carolyn's preschool, Let's Be Friends, where Samantha was going to help the toddlers do arts and crafts. Joe was already at work, so Samantha and I were home alone. When I walked into my bathroom, I fell, because the bathroom floor was slippery. I tried to grab on to the sink so I wouldn't fall, or at least to break my fall, but the sink was slippery, too. So I fell onto the floor, landing on my side and rear-end. I thanked God that I did not hurt anything except for my butt!

Samantha was in her bedroom getting ready, and she heard me fall. She ran out of her bedroom so fast to make sure I wasn't hurt: when she saw me on the floor, she asked, "Mommy, are you OK?" I was really angry and fed up with myself and with life's ordeal: I felt like I had reached my boiling point over everything I had endured since the aneurysm burst in my head when I was 14 years old. I was so extremely mad, and I said so many negative things about my situation. But when I saw the look in Samantha's eyes and how worried she was for her Mommy, I became really disappointed and upset with myself. As her mother, I am supposed to be her example, to show her that I'm strong and that I can overcome my situation one way or another. But those feelings of anger overtook my heart, and that's when I realized my soul and spirit were totally drained and I was extremely exhausted with myself. I just wanted to close my eyes and go to another place in my mind where I wouldn't be scared anymore of what unexpected challenges I might face in the future.

Samantha tried to help me up off the bathroom floor, but she couldn't. She was just a little girl: she shouldn't have to be able to lift her mother off the floor! I told her, "Samantha, you can't get me up; Mommy is too big for you, Honey."

That's when I completely broke down: I started bawling, with tears streaming down my face, and I blurted out, "Why is everything in my life so horribly *hard*? Why, God? No matter what I do with my disability, it's just so strenuous and grueling." Then I realized what I was saying and how it might affect Samantha, who was still trying to help me up, so I stopped expressing my frustration out loud so I wouldn't upset Samantha. But I still thought to myself, *I'm getting tired of being so patient with myself and living like this, not being able to bend my legs. I keep falling and losing my balance all the time, not being able to walk, or get dressed, or even take a shower. No matter what I do, I am so limited. What's this all about, God? What's my purpose?*

I kept repeating that over and over again in my mind, while at the same time, I felt my stomach being twisted, as though my core of power and strength was breaking apart. All I wanted to do was to scream my heart out and quit! I kept telling God, *"My life is so horribly hard! I'm just done!"* But deep down, I was hoping my cry would reach to the heavens and be heard by God and that his angels would lift me up with their wings and give me the strength to find my way back to my heart.

After I took control of my frustration a few moments later, I calmed down in front of Samantha because I realized I needed to be strong for her. I said, "Give me a hug, Sweets! I'm just having a rough morning, Samantha, but it's OK now, I'll stop crying. I am so sorry, Beautiful, I will defeat this! Your hug is making me feel better!" Then I felt this comforting feeling in my heart: I understood that it was important for me to be strong for her, and I realized I needed to take control of my actions and words in front of Samantha. Then I closed my eyes and felt a whisper from within that God and the angels had heard me. I felt as though I was hearing, *It's OK, don't get discouraged, and always believe and have faith! Don't let your anger and frustration and self-pity get the best of you* .I realized I need to carry on and focus on the positive things in my life, not the negative, because I am so blessed!

Then I opened my eyes taking all the power within my heart that I needed to keep on fighting and to not be afraid. I accepted that it is up to me to make my life however I want it to be! I have God, the Archangel Michael, and the other angels right beside me every step of the way! So I asked Samantha to bring me the phone. She ran as quickly as she could to call Mom-Mom and Pop-Pop. Joe's parents rushed over right away: it seemed they were there in the blink of an eye. When they saw me on the bathroom floor, they tried to make my situation lighter and not as intense and difficult, so they started saying silly things to make Samantha and me laugh. And it worked!

Then Mom got in front of me and Dad got in back of me and Mom said, "On the count of three, we'll get you up." Dad said okay, they counted together one-two-three, and they got me up. We all yelled, *Yay!* After they got me up, Dad was trying to be silly again, but I tried to hold back from laughing. "Dad, don't make me laugh, because I really, *really* have to tinkle!" They laughed and said, "Okay, let's hurry and get out of here."

A little while later, I dropped off Samantha at the Let's Be Friends School, and I went straight to the LA Fitness gym. As soon as I walked in, one of the trainers I knew helped me on the leg press right away. Chris was always so sweet to me, and he knew exactly how to help me get me on the machine. I started my work out and did 130 leg presses, 10 or 20 at a time, with 90 pounds of weight. I love doing this machine because after I do the leg presses, my heart beats so fast, which gives me such a high: I can imagine that I'm actually running through the farm fields, as I did when I was a little girl. That is the greatest feeling!

After I finished on the leg-press machine, I had to go to the bathroom. I got myself into the handicapped stall, grabbed onto the bar to lift myself up from my scooter, and swiveled my feet around so I would be able to shut the bathroom stall door. Then I grabbed onto the scooter to get in front of the toilet, but my legs lost balance, and I fell right onto the bathroom floor. I couldn't believe I had fallen *again* and that I was lying on the floor of the bathroom at LA Fitness! I was in complete shock, thinking, *I am so tired of living my life like this.*

Then I heard someone ask me, "Are you OK?" There was another woman in the bathroom, and she had heard me fall. My voice was shaky, and I was trying to hold back tears, but I said, "No, I'm not OK. Please, can you help me?" She came in to help me off the floor, and she asked me again if I was OK, and this time I said yes. But I just couldn't hold my tears back any longer. I started wailing and saying, "I am so tired of living like this! This is the second time today I've fallen! I fell in my own bathroom earlier this morning, and now I've fallen again. I can't believe this is happening to me."

Then she bent down next to me and put her arm around me floor and also to make me feel more comfortable. She told me her name was Mary Ellen, and she said in a caring, soft voice, "I know this must be so hard for you. But I see you here all the time, and you don't give up." I was still crying hard, with tears coming down my face, and I said, "I just want to give up! I'm tired!" She said again, "You *can't* Give up. You inspire me, and you inspire so many people here because we admire the power you have to not give up on yourself. You give *us* that power, not to give up on *ourselves*!" When she said that, my tears stopped.

She held my hand really tightly and asked if she could try to help me up. I told her there was no way she would be able to get me up because I knew my body had become too rigid and my legs were like a stiff board. I knew I would just be dead weight, and as a result, there would be no way she would be able to get me off the floor. I told her she would need to get help, and I assured her I would be OK while she went for help. So Mary Ellen left and came back with another girl named Paige, who worked at the gym.

When they came into the bathroom to help me, though, I knew right away that even the two of them wouldn't be able to get me off the floor because my feelings of frustration and embarrassment were so intense that my legs had gotten even stiffer. I knew there was no way I would be able to bend them, not even an inch. I had to relax first, and that was so hard to do through this whole ordeal. I told them I knew they wouldn't be able to move me because I was too stiff, and I said they needed to get one of the trainers. So Paige stayed with me to calm me down, and Mary Ellen went to go get help.

Then my close friend Karrie walked in the bathroom and saw me in the stall on the floor. When she saw that I had been crying, Karrie said she would help me get up, but I told her the same thing I had told Paige and Mary Ellen, that I was too stiff. Then I started to feel sorry for myself again, and I started crying and saying, "I can't believe this happened again." I told Karrie I had fallen earlier at home, and now again at the gym, and Karrie soothed me and got me to stop crying.

A few minutes later, three of the male trainers walked into the bathroom to help me up from in the stall. Ron, Chris, and Kyle are terrific, dedicated trainers, they understand my situation, and they give me so much support whenever I need their help! They really are incredible. Nevertheless, when I looked up at them from the floor of the women's bathroom stall, I thought to myself, *"Oh my Gosh, am I in a very bad dream!" I have three men here to help me to get me up from a bathroom stall."* I was so ashamed of myself that I broke down and started crying again. Ron said, "It's OK, Theresa, we've got you!" I wasn't only embarrassed; I was also worried that my falling in the bathroom would cause problems for me coming to the gym in the future, so I asked Ron about that. He said, "Don't even think that! We are so proud of you of always being here and do what you do. We are always here for you!"

Then Ron got on one side of me and Chris got on my other side while Kyle tried to get the scooter out of the way because there wasn't much room for maneuvering to get me up. It took a few moments to figure out how they were going to do this. Chris said, "Hold onto us real tight, while we get you up!" Even with all their combined strength, getting me up required lots of effort on their behalf because my body was so stiff and rigid. They tried to get me back into my scooter, but they couldn't because my legs wouldn't bend. I decided to stand next to my scooter and relax first; then my body and legs would be easier to move and I might be able to bend my legs a bit.

Then Karrie walked over to me to hold my hand and make sure I was steady and safe on my feet. When the trainers made sure I was OK and left the bathroom, Mary Ellen, Paige, and Karrie were going to stay with me until I was ready to leave the bathroom. I told them they did not need to stay with me: I assured them I was fine, and I thanked them for all their help. "You all are so sweet!" Then Karrie said, "I'm basically done my workout, so I'll wait for you, Theresa." I told her that it would take me a few minutes because I still had to go to the bathroom and then get back into my scooter." She said, "That's fine. I'll wait!"

Karrie saw the unsettled look on my face and how troubled I was from within. She squeezed my hand and said, "Theresa, take a deep breath. Don't you realize when other people see you here, you give them a reason to work out, Theresa? You inspire them to not give up on themselves because most people here know how dedicated you are and what struggles and difficulties you have in your life. They see you don't get discouraged from what you want to do." Then Karrie looked at me with a beautiful, glowing smile on her face and said, "They think you are just like the Energizer Bunny, Theresa. You don't stop, and you don't give up! YOU keep going and going and going. So, after you're finished here in the bathroom, let's do the arm machines together."

I *so* appreciated her pep talk and the kind words she said about me and my efforts at the gym. Still, my first reaction was to say, "I'll pass on the arm machines: I just want to get out of here and pretend this never happened." Then I reconsidered. I thought *I can't just give up!* I knew Karrie was right, so I said to her, "I changed my mind. That will be GREAT!" And a few minutes later, we were back in the gym, working out. That was a hard day for me, but the people who came to my rescue were all so kind and supportive. They helped me not only by picking me up but by restoring my faith in others and in myself.

*   *   *   *   *

My precious Samantha is also a great help to me, in so many ways. For instance, it's really hard for me to lie down on the couch because my legs don't bend easily. They don't bend on their own, so I have to *make* them bend, and that takes me a while. I have to lift one leg onto the sofa and then swing my body so my other leg can get up. When Samantha is home, she usually helps me. She'll say, "I can help you, Mommy, I like doing it for you." She struggles a bit—after all, she's only 8years old at the time I'm writing this—but she can do it. And she puts a pillow under my head, so I'll be extra comfortable. She does this so often for me that she's started to think of it as her job; in fact, she thinks I can't do it without her. So one night when Samantha came home from her gymnastics class and saw me lying on the couch, she asked me, "How did you do that without me?" She was so surprised: I could see it on her face.

Samantha goes to gymnastics twice a week. She's done it since she was two or three years old. Samantha is incredible: she can do cartwheels, front walkovers, backbends, the balance beam, uneven bars, parallel bars, everything. She even got a trampoline for Christmas from Joe's parents. She also wants to take dance lessons, but she does so much now. She plays guitar, the violin, and chimes, and she's a Girl Scout. She's in 4th grade now. She's so funny, and I love her to pieces.

Joe always figures out a way for me to be included in everything. Samantha, Joe, and I went sledding when she was about five years old: Joe put Samantha and me on a great big sled, we had so much fun, and his parents took pictures of us. Soon after we met, Joe figured out how I could get around on the beach, so we enjoy that in the summertime. Even at an amusement park, he includes me. I can't go on the rides, because it would take me forever to get up on them. But most of the time, Joe takes Samantha on the rides and I stay down below, and they always call out to me, "Hi, Mommy!!!!!"

Lots of times, Joe carried me onto the rides. When we went to Disneyworld a few years ago, he carried me everywhere; I can't believe he did that, because sometimes he carried me quite a distance. Then Samantha saw how much he was carrying me, so Joe carried her sometimes, so she wouldn't become jealous of me. I don't know how he did that, but I certainly know I'm blessed.

Even though I know I'm blessed, sometimes I get angry or frustrated that I even need someone to help me all the time. I know this was God's plan, for me to meet Joe, and I'm so fortunate that we've been happily married for 20 years. He's so nice and understanding of me, when I'm so frustrated and torn by what I can't do by myself. Sometimes I lash out and I'm not so nice. It's no excuse, but I just get tired at moments like these. I end up breaking from within through my life's ordeal and all I wish for is to be completely independent. I'm not really angry with him, I'm just frustrated with my situation. I Love Him So Much!

I'm also lucky to have Joe's parents in my life: they're so good to me, and I don't know what I'll do as they get older. I try not to think about that, because losing my own parents was so difficult for me. After my father died in 2002, my mother sold the house we had all grown up in, and she moved into the house that had belonged to my grandmother. As the years were passing by, my Mother was getting respiratory problems and it was getting worse throughout time. It was so bad that my Mother ended up using a breathing machine, while she was sleeping at night. So one day, her breathing was so unbearable and extremely excruciating that the person who was with her that day called the ambulance and they rushed her to the hospital right away. When it was time for her to leave the Hospital weeks later, my brothers and sisters and I were trying to get nurses or aides to help care for her. But she continued to decline. I did not take any classes in the fall semester of 2013, because my mom wasn't doing very well. She was in such pain, and she did not want to eat. She was having a really difficult time talking and breathing: when she talked, the words came out as a mumble and nothing but a whisper.

One day, though, she somehow found the strength to talk to me loud and clear because she desperately wanted me to understand what she wanted to tell me. My heart was overwhelmed by how clearly she spoke that day. She asked me, "Theresa, have you been to DuPont Hospital recently?" I said I hadn't, and she said, "Go back: don't ever give up on a place where you love to be" I told her, "Mommy, I'll always be devoted to DuPont. That's our place, right?" She said, "Yes, doll," while she was trying so hard to keep her eyes open.

Then she asked me, "How is your book coming along?" I told her it was almost done. She said, "Don't give up on your book. Don't give up, Beautiful, get it done." I said, "Mommy, I'll get it done; I never give up. I learned that from you and Daddy. That's a precious gift, a quality that you and Daddy gave me, right, Mommy?" She just smiled, and I laughed even as tears fell down my cheeks.

While she was talking to me, I moved up to the edge of my scooter seat and I grabbed her hand and squeezed it really tightly, and then I put my head down on her shoulder. I leaned against her bed, trying to hold myself back from crying, even though I already was. She said, "I love you, Theresa. I love you, and don't ever forget that." After she said that to me, I was sobbing so much, while hiding my face in her shoulder because I did not want her to see the tears coming down my face. Then I found the strength to get up out of my scooter, and I wrapped my arms around her, really tightly, not wanting to let her go. The pain in my heart was completely excruciating: I felt like my heart was being ripped out of my body, knowing that my mother was going to pass away. Then she whispered in my ear, "I love you, Theresa, and I'll always be proud of you. Be happy, beautiful!"

What my mother said to me that day will always be with me: she gave me a golden treasure that will always stay in my heart forever!!!

A few days later, it was Joann's and my Birthday. My Mother would always go way beyond to do her best to make it so special for both of us. She would get a huge Italian Rum Cake for each of us because she knew how much we loved it. Also, she would try her hardest to get us together to celebrate it somehow, someway because our Mother knew how much it meant for the both of us. She would shower us with all her love, excitement, happiness, and gifts. A couple of days before she passed away, on the morning of my Birthday, I went into her Hospital room, and saw my Mother's eyes were close. Aunt Jenny, Aunt Joe, Grace, Joann, and Christine were around her bed with this big huge Italian Rum Birthday cake and gifts. Which, I was told by Christine my Mother got our birthday gifts before she got sick because she was always afraid she was going to die. Seeing all this and knowing what she did for us. My heart just dropped and I was so flustered. I was totally beside myself with a pounding heart, tears coming down my face. I completely did not expect to see that because My Mother was in so much pain and agony. Then my eyes looked up to the heavens and I said to myself, "My Mother is unbelievable, you can't take her, God!" My heart was wrenching and being ripped out because still she was doing her absolute best to make Joann's Birthday and mine so very special. I went up to her Bed with a shivering lip, I held her hand very tight, and I said, "Mommy, You so and still are unbelievable!" "You tickle me so much, Mommy - with a sly giggle. Then I squeezed her hand even tighter with my sopping eyes and with a shaky voice. Then I tried to edge up on her bed, went up to her ear, and whispered, "You put such Beautiful Stars in my Heart, Mommy, you are so incredible! I love you so much! I love you." She heard me, and then she winked her eyes at me and gave me a Beautiful smile!

*   *   *   *   *

The morning before my mom passed away, the telephone rang, and Joe picked it up and handed it to me. It was my sister Marie, and she told me to get to the hospital right away. She said the doctors had put a breathing tube down Mommy's throat, attached to a ventilator, because she was no longer able to breathe on her own. The doctors wanted all of us at the hospital because they want us all to be there when they pull out the tube. Once that happened, Mommy would be able to pass away peacefully and have no more agonizing pain and suffering.

When she said that to me, my heart dropped so deep within me, I began bawling my eyes out, and I screamed, "NO, MARIE! WE CAN'T DO THAT!" Marie said, "Theresa, it's time." I said, "MOMMY CAN'T DIE." But Marie said, "Theresa, you need to be there for Mommy: She is in so much pain and you can't think about yourself, you have to think about Mommy and want she wants. Mommy loves you so much, and she wants you to be strong. You can do this for Mommy."

After I got off the phone with my sister, my heart was trembling and shaken with such a jolt. It was like a bomb went off and blew my heart into thousands of pieces and there was no way to put them back together again. Joe held me very tight and told me, "Compose yourself, and be strong, Theresa. It's time."

Joe and I rushed to the hospital, and when we got to the third floor, I saw that most of my loved ones were already assembled in the intensive care waiting room for my mother. They were taking turns, going two at a time to her room to sit at Mommy's bedside. Each one of us wanted to be with her as much as we could because we knew we had precious little time left with her. When I went into her room, Grace and Andy were with her. My mother was in such a deep sleep, and I knew the ventilator was the only thing keeping her alive. I was so distressed to see this, and it was so incredibly hard to hold myself back from crying. My heart and mind were so lost and confused. Being there just did not seem real to me, that this was actually happening. I kept thinking that this was a horrible and atrocious nightmare and that I would wake up from it, but I knew deep down that wasn't going to happen.

I thought about all the things my mother did for me throughout my life: she went way beyond the call of duty. I can never express what my heart wants to say. She was more to me than the word "Mother" means. I was struggling so hard to hold strong, then I gathered all my strength and wheeled close to her bed with my scooter very carefully, with Andy's help, because I did not want to hit any of the machines that were keeping her alive or taking away her pain. Then I reached out, grabbed my mother's hand, and said, "I love you, Mommy." I said it over and over, but the more I said it, the more excruciating it was. Then I saw tears in Andy's eyes, and that is when the pain in my heart overtook my strength and I couldn't hold on any longer. I put my head down on her bed, not wanting

Mommy, Grace, or Andy to see me crying over how much I did not want to let her go. At the same time, I was squeezing Mommy's hand tighter and tighter.

After a bit, I found the courage from within not to cry, and I lifted my head. With tears still coming down my face, sobbing quietly to myself, I tried to tell her, "Mommy, I love you so much. You can let go now and be with Daddy. It's ok; I'll be strong. You gave me that strength, you embedded so much of your love, faith, determination, and power in my heart to believe that I can overcome anything that is in my way. That's why I became the person of who I am today, Mommy. I am never going to give up, never!" I was trying so hard not to lose myself in my tears, but that wasn't happening, so I laid my head down, hiding my face while trying to compose myself. Then I lifted my head up again and said, "I will always make you proud! MOMMY, YOU HEAR ME. I'LL ALWAYS MAKE YOU PROUD!"

Then I found the power to struggle up from my scooter, and I leaned against her bed and held my mom really tightly. *I did not want to let her go!* I was trying to hide my tears in her shoulder, but my quiet crying suddenly got louder and louder. When I became aware of that, I gave her my blessing to pass away: I knew that very soon, she would no longer be here with me and my Mother would be going to a place in heaven with Daddy, with other loved ones, and with God!

During the hours while we were all waiting for my mother to pass away, the pain in our hearts was getting more and more unbearable to deal with. We all knew the inevitable was coming soon, and we all had to agree when to pull out the breathing tube. I vividly remember seeing some of my nieces and my nephew Nicolas (John and Lauri's son) coming into my mother's room and surrounding her bed. They were also crying, and they kept saying, "We love you, Mom-Mom! WE LOVE YOU!" Then my niece Christine (Marie's daughter) went over to the bed, leaned over and wiped her grandmother's mouth, all the while looking at the monitors.

When unexpectedly the ventilator's alarm went off, everyone got so fearful and apprehensive. We weren't sure what was happening! In a flash, a nurse walked in to see if the equipment was still doing what it was supposed to do—which it was. After the nurse checked the ventilator and reassured us, she then left the room. Nicolas held onto my mother's bedrail, and Melina (Grace and Luis's daughter) fixed my mother's hair with her fingers because she knew how much Mom-Mom loved to get her hair done and all "prettied up." Then all of the grandchildren started to recall memories from when they were kids, and they were talking directly to their grandmother: "Mom-Mom, remember the times when we were all at the farm, playing with all the kitty-cats, and having family parties during the summer?" "Remember the big barbecues with lots of food, when we ate outside, at the picnic table underneath your favorite tree?"

Then Rosie (Rose and Jeff's daughter) got on one side of the bed and Natalie (John and Lauri's daughter) got on the other, and both were holding Mom-Mom's hands. Rosie spoke up and said, "Mom-Mom, remember the time Natalie and I were real little at the farmhouse, having a barbecue, and we put Joann's cat Jasmine in the toilet because we wanted to give him a bath?" Natalie added, "When we got him out of the toilet, he looked like a drowned rat." They laughed, even while tears were rolling down their cheeks. At the same time, Andrea (Andy's and Kim's daughter) and Marisa (Grace and Luis's daughter) were trying so hard to hold their tears back; then Andrea said, "You got crazy and silly grandkids, Mom-Mom!" She laughed and chuckled, trying to be funny and making light of things, because what was happening was so overwhelmingly sad. Then Marisa wiped her eyes, took a deep breath, and said, "What about the time when Melina put gum in Nicolas's hair, and it was so tangled up that there was no way to get it out, so my Mom—or maybe it was Mom-Mom—had to cut it out." Then Nicolas said, "I think it was Aunt Grace who cut it out of my hair. All I remember is that a lot was chopped off."

It got quiet again, and all we heard was the breathing machine. Then, suddenly, my mother opened her eyes, as if to let us all know she was still there and that she was listening. Rosie's buoyant voice said, "Mom-Mom can hear us! She can hear us!" Next Melina said, with a loving look and tears in her eyes, "I don't have any doubt that she didn't hear us!" All the grandchildren started talking then: "That's our Mom-Mom. "She doesn't miss a thing." "She always wants to get into the middle of the action. Right, Mom-Mom?" "We love you!" That's when I knew, from a whisper within my mother, that *she absolutely felt the infinite love of her grandchildren.* Everyone who was in her room was in complete awe: when she opened her eyes, it was like a burst of a beautiful glow in all our hearts.

* * * * *

It was in the evening around 6:00 when the time came to pull out the respirator in my mother's throat. When I heard the doctor tell us this, my heart was pounding wildly, and so was everybody else's. I couldn't believe this would be the last time I would see my mother alive. I couldn't accept that I was not going to hear her tender voice telling me how proud she was of me and her encouraging words telling me to be happy when I have my rough and bad days. I was trying to grasp the idea that I wasn't going to feel her warm and loving touch or have her arms wrapped around Samantha or me when she gave us hugs and kisses. There would be no more giving her a call every night telling her how much we love her and wishing her sweet dreams. It just did not seem real to me; my heart was literally wrenching with so much agony. I kept looking at the clock desperately counting every moment before the doctors came into the room.

Then a bit of time passed, and the doctors and nurses walked into her room. I was literally shaking. They told us it was time, and they asked us to get the others who were in the waiting room. My sister Marie went and got, Julius, John, and the rest of my brothers and sisters and my mother's sisters and their kids. Then the doctors explained that she would be well sedated with a great amount of morphine, so when they take out the respirator, she wouldn't feel a thing and she would pass away peacefully, without pain.

We all gathered around my mother's bed. When the nurse began removing her respirator, it was tremendously distressing to watch. At first, my mother started gagging and couldn't get her breath. Immediately, the nurse increased her morphine, and soon after, it looked like my mother was more serene and calm. The minutes slipped away as we waited for my mother's passing and savored every last moment with her.

Then unexpectedly, she opened her eyes, and we all started talking to her, saying "We love you, Mommy! We love you!" My Aunt Jenny and Aunt Joe were saying "Rose, we love you!" Then my sister Grace said, "It's OK, Mommy. It's OK: Daddy is waiting for you." At the same time, Grace was holding my mother's hand very tightly, and tears were streaming down her face.

I was literally lost within myself, waiting for the inevitable to come. I was beside my mother, standing on one side of her bed while holding tightly to my brother Jimmy. I was crying, and I tried to bury my face in his shoulder, closing my eyes and wishing for a miracle.

Then I looked up and saw my sister Rose seeing how much pain she had in her heart, sobs of tears pouring down her face telling my Mother, I love you, I love you, Mommy. I reached my hand out to her and I held Rose's hand real tight and I kept squeezing it tighter and tighter not wanting to let it go. Shortly, a few moments later, I saw Joann, crying. She leaned over in front of my mother, whose beautiful hazel eyes was fixed on looking at her. Then suddenly my Mother moved her eyes around on all of us. The look she gave was unforgettable to me because it was such a shimmering, glassy and gaze look of such entwine energy of love for us all. That is when I felt an overwhelming comforting of love, and I knew that was my mother's way of telling us, that she is proud of us and she loves us all very much, she will always be in our hearts!

Then we all reached out, and we all held one another's hands and we all joined in. As we said the prayer of Our Father, I could feel the beautiful tranquility and the true essence of our mother: it was a very powerful feeling. I will always remember those last moments with my mother: they will live on in my heart forever!

My mother died on December 2, 2013. My heart was heavy with deep sadness and grief. In her passing, I realized what she went through with me. I felt so much pain, agony, and heartbreak of seeing someone I loved so much with all my heart, and all the praying in the world couldn't stop the pain my mother had to endure. As the days grew into weeks, she improved a bit and I believed my prayers was answered. Then she declined again. But I still hoped she would beat this. Weeks became months, and I still believed she was going to be OK because I recognized what courage and strength she had, and I tried so hard to have that with her. While she was holding on in her final days, I did not want to let her go; I was afraid she would leave me and I wanted so badly not to leave her. The pain in my heart was so beyond measure: it was excruciating. I wasn't thinking of her pain, how much she was suffering. I kept thinking of myself; I wasn't ready to comprehend yet that she might die. I realize I was being selfish and I did not want to hear from any family members telling me otherwise. I was just so horribly angry. I just did not want to accept it. But with faith, belief and trusting in God, I knew deep down in my heart that letting my mother go was the right decision but the most difficult one.

I wanted to find the most powerful and potent words to say how much my mother meant to me. So I could tell each and every person at her funeral how much I cherished the great impact my mother had on my life. I also wanted everyone to know how precious and beautiful my mother really was and still is in the Heavenly Heavens! This is what I wrote, from the feelings deep within my heart, and I read it in church at my mother's funeral:

"I will always remember my beautiful mother: I loved her so very much, and I always will. She was so incredibly outstanding and remarkable. She overcame so many obstacles that were thrown at her, and she did it with a smile. She achieved so much in her lifetime. She was a remarkable daughter, sister, wife, mother, grandmother, and great-grandmother. In raising her 10 children, you can only imagine the sacrifices she made and the selflessness she had. She always gave to us first and thought of herself last.

"My heart is breaking into bits and pieces, and it is going to be so hard for me to put them back together again, but I know without a doubt that she is in better hands with God. She will always be alive in my heart; her spirit will always be with me, guiding me every step of the way. My dear and beautiful mother embedded in me so many incredible, powerful, and nurturing qualities— qualities I've tried to bestow on my own daughter, Samantha.

"My mother never left my side and always gave me tremendous and endless love, hope, and encouragement. She always told me, "Theresa, be happy." She was so proud of me. She taught me to have faith, to believe in myself, and to be proud of who I am. She ignited that flame within me to find my strength and power, to keep on fighting, to never give up on my heart's dreams and myself—to believe that they can and will come true, one way or another.

"My mother made me realize I have that power in my hands that it's up to me to make the best of what I have, so that I can achieve whatever I want to have a happy, successful, fulfilling life!

That is why I have come as far as I have and have become the person I am today. If it weren't for my mother, I know—without a doubt in my mind—that my heart, my spirit, my perseverance, and my determination wouldn't be as strong as they are today! My mother was *my rock*, and now she will always be *my bright and beautiful star!!!* I looked up to the heavens with a deep heavy heart and tears in my eyes. Then I had an overwhelming sense—a whisper from within—that my mother told me to live my life on my terms and live life to the fullest and be happy! I embraced her words so dearly in my heart, and I answered her in my thoughts: *That is what I am absolutely going to do! I'm never, never going to give up. I'll always make you proud!!!"* Then I reached my hand up and I blew her a kiss and said,

"I Love You, Mommy!"

WHATEVER TOMORROW BRINGS, I AM never letting go and I won't be shaken from my strength of Perseverance, Motivation, and Determination that was embedded inside me. I will always keep pushing forward with God's help and hold on tight within my heart's power of my learning lessons, the healing of my soul, my life experiences, God's incredible love, and His amazing words that are "A Whisper From Within." His wonderful power up above in the Beautiful Heavenly Heavens had given me the strength to rise with the utmost intention. Seeing, the overall clear pictures of wisdom and knowledge, so that I can conquer my disability, overcome the hurdles and obstacles that confront me every day, and keep pursuing what was meant for me to do in this lifetime of mine, one way or the other..........

Even, if my spirit is failing at times, God will give me the strength to pick myself up at those moments. I will lift my hands up to Him and do my extreme best because I will always Believe, have Faith and Never have Doubt. I will always hold onto His love and never let go of the Incredible Heaven and the Amazing Earth; with everything in my power I can Prevail, Reach for the Unreachable and believe that the word Possible is Never Impossible!!!

AS I WAS ENDING THIS book about my life, a new chapter is starting. I found out that I have Breast Cancer, the next battle and hurdle in my life is beginning. As I push through my next obstacle, I will use all my strength and courage to overcome. Holding on to God Almighty in my heart, knowing that I'm not alone and I will defeat this and become the next Breast Cancer Survivor!

CPSIA information can be obtained
at www.ICGtesting.com
Printed in the USA
FFOW04n1400290915
17301FF